Truer Grit

by

John R. Huckaby

PITTSBURGH, PENNSYLVANIA 15222

The contents of this work including, but not limited to, the accuracy of events, people, and places depicted; opinions expressed; permission to use previously published materials included; and any advice given or actions advocated are solely the responsibility of the author, who assumes all liability for said work and indemnifies the publisher against any claims stemming from publication of the work.

All Rights Reserved
Copyright © 2012 by John R. Huckaby

No part of this book may be reproduced or transmitted, downloaded, distributed, reverse engineered, or stored in or introduced into any information storage and retrieval system, in any form or by any means, including photocopying and recording, whether electronic or mechanical, now known or hereinafter invented without permission in writing from the publisher.

RoseDog Books
701 Smithfield Street
Pittsburgh, PA 15222
Visit our website at *www.rosedogbookstore.com*

ISBN: 978-1-4349-8995-6
eISBN: 978-1-4349-7987-2

This book was made possible because of John's wife who typed the manuscript and devoted great amounts of time in the preparation of the text and proof reading.

CONTENTS

Foreward: RUNNING RESUME vii
INTRODUCTION ix
PREFACE xi
PRESS RELEASE xiii
PARADISE xv

Book One

CHAPTER 1 THE HUCKABYS SINCE 1764 1
CHAPTER 2 AGE 12 TO 19 (YOUTH TO NAVY ENLISTMENT) 4

Book Two

CHAPTER 3 US NAVY JUNE 14, 1940 TO JUNE 14, 1946 9

Book Three

CHAPTER 4 END OF WWII AND START OF KOREA WAR 19
JOHN'S ACTIVE MILITARY SERVICE (WEDNESDAY NIGHTS) BETWEEN JUNE 1946 AND JUNE 1950 19
MY DAYTIME JOBS BETWEEN JUNE 1946 AND JUNE 1950 (END OF WWII TO START OF THE KOREAN WAR) 19
MY PART TIME JOB BETWEEN JUNE 1946 AND JUNE 1950 (END OF WWII AND START OF KOREAN WAR) 20
MY FOUR YEAR STUDY AND COMPLETION OF COURSE AT THE LONG BEACH ACADEMY OF ART (MONDAY AND FRIDAY NIGHTS) FROM JUNE 1946 TO JUNE 1950 (END OF WWII TO START OF KOREA) 20

Book Four

CHAPTER 5 23

Book Five

CHAPTER 6 MERCHANT MARINES WORLD TRAVLES 27

Book Six

Philco, July 5, 1955-1967 31

Book Seven

- CHAPTER 7 SUMMARY OF ULTRAMARATHONS 35
- CHAPTER 8 "The Athens International Peace Marathon" 39
- CHAPTER 9 "The Ultimate Challenge" 41
- CHAPTER 10 INTERESTING HIGHLIGHTS OF THE TRIATHLON 46
- CHAPTER 11 BOSTON MARATHON (4 TIMES) 50
- CHAPTER 12 MEMPHIS RUNNING MADNESS 55
- CHAPTER 13 MIDNIGHT SUN RACE ** NORTH POLE 59
- CHAPTER 14 1981 MARION CORRIGAN MEMORIAL 24 HOUR SUPER RUN, AUBURN, NEW YORK (NOVEMBER 21-22, 1981) 61
- CHAPTER 15 MONTAUK TO MANHATTEN ** RUNNING ODYSSEY 64
- CHAPTER 16 THE FIRST 60KM CANANDAIGUA LAKE FALL CLASSIC "A DEVIL OF A GOOD RUN" 69
- CHAPTER 17 NOVEMBER 7, 1982 ERIE CANAL RUN 60KM 71
- CHAPTER 18 JOHN HUCKABY'S HEARTATTACK 73

Book Eight

- CHAPTER 19 ELECTRONIC ADJUNCT MOHAWK VALLEY COMMUNITY COLLEGE 1960 77
- CHAPTER 20 JOHN R. HUCKABY ART CAREER 81

- APPENDIX #1 COMPLETED ULTRA MARATHONS, MARATHONS 107
- APPENDIX #2 John R. Huckaby's wartime and cold war experiences 109
- APENDIX #3 John R. Huckaby and Family Photographs/ages 35 to 95 111

RUNNING RESUME

December 3, 1981

John Huckaby, known as "The Incredible Huck" was born in the little cow town of Ranger, Texas over 60 years ago. As a boy he chased road runners, coyotes, sage hens and Jack rabbits. Huck is a computer engineer and employed at Griffith Air force base near Rome, NY. He lives in a resort park with his wife Betty, his 96 year old mother in law and his Marathon poodle Suzette, his jogging companion.

    Ten years ago he was rejected from a heart screening test and given a life expectancy of less than six months. It was suggested, "See your lawyer and make out your will before you see your doctor and take it easy." Instead Huck changed his life style and started jogging up the ladder to become a fitness animal. Under the direction of his coach Tom Hovey and trainer Rome's Mayor, Carl Eilenberg, he became a legend.

    In the past seven years Huck has run over 24,000 miles. The distance of around the world at the equator, and has completed 119 standard 26.2 mile marathons and 31 ultra marathons. Along the way he's lost four chins and 85 pounds, his size 46 shorts no longer fit, and his blood pressure and pulse rate has been halved. Huck is a living example of what diet and exercise can do. Some of his feats include:

    *Running the original Pheidippides Marathon in Athens, Greece three times nonstop. A distance of 78.6 miles to prove himself three times greater than the best Greek runner Pheidippides who died after running it only once.

    *July 5, 1981 he ran the North pole ultra marathon form the last Eskimo village of Nanisivik to Arctic bay, 52.4 miles over a 6,700 foot glacier where the polar bear roams.

    *In 1980 Huck was featured in Ripley's Believe it or not for completing the premier endurance event of the world, the Hawaiian Triathlon. At 60 he swam 2.4 miles in open seas, biked 112 mountainous miles and caped it off with a 26.2 mile marathon.

    *Halloween weekend 1980 Huck ran 109 miles in the goblin gallop, completing a 2.5 mile, a 10KM, a 12 hour and a 24 hour ultra marathon all nonstop back to back in Memphis, Tenn.

    *Huck in 1980 ran the Boston Marathon four times (104.8 miles) nonstop to protest against unfair qualifying standards for women and men runners in the masters age groups. They were changed favorably.

    *In April 1981 he ran the Albany to Boston Ultra marathon, a 205 mile zigzag course over the Berkshire Mountains in 71 hours, with the last leg the Boston Marathon itself.

    *Huck ran the western states 100 mile ultimate challenge over the high Sierra Mountains on July 7, 1979. It's like running up and down the Empire state building 20 times while covering 100 miles.

    *In 1982 he ran a three day, 160 mile odyssey from Montauk Point lighthouse across Long Island to Staten Island and then completed the New York City marathon course.

    *On October 4, 1981 Huck became the National Road Runners Club of America US National champion for 100KM (62 miles) for the over 60 age group.

    *November 21, 1981 John Huckaby ran 1,088 laps around a 150 meter track and covered 101 miles, 754 yards to become national champ for his age bracket of 60 plus for the 100 mile and 24 hour distances and perhaps set world standards for those distances?

    Huck's future plans are for a transam run from L.A. to New York City from sea to shining sea, over 3,000 miles in 77 days.

INTRODUCTION

Self Actualizing in the later years: A portrait of John R. Huckaby by Anna Behrens

One picture, so it is said, is worth a thousand words. This book of Incredible Huck has been compiled to support my theory- a theory that growing old, even in our youth glorifying society, need not be a terrible nor terrifying experience. The latter years of a person's life can be just as, or even more, productive than the years of his youth. Furthermore, I believe that this is so, not because of chance, but because certain individuals have a zeal or lust for life throughout their lives. The latter years, especially the way our economic system is set up, often provides the time (retirement) and finances (pensions), saving plans that allow a creative older person to draw on his experiences, achievements and talents to produce even more than he did in youth. What I am saying basically, is that if a person chooses to be fully alive and involved in life through the use of all his gifts, this need not end, but rather become enhanced by aging. On the other hand, if a person decides early in life not to participate and simply let "life pass him by," this is the individual one will find in the rocking chair waiting to die.

My theory is supported in particular by two psychologists- one very famous and the other not so well known, Abraham Maslow, in his book <u>Motivation and Personality</u> (2nd edition, 1970), outlines his famous Hierarchy of needs. The need for self actualization is the need he lists last, and is the one which he feels flowers in the personality after the other, more basic needs have been satisfied (ie: food, clothing, shelter, safety, love, self esteem). Self actualization is a process whereby an individual attempts to fulfill himself by becoming all that he knows or believes that he can possibly become; he tries to make full use of all his gifts and abilities, both physical and mental. For example, a dancer would start out early in life learning the craft, perhaps try out for parts in school productions, join a college dance troupe, perhaps become famous, get into show business and in later years, set up his own dance programs of teaching. In every phase, the person would be using his gifts and talents to their full potential or at least, he would be attempting to do so, he would be living life to the fullest: he would be a self actualizing person. This desire to self actualize. I believe, is stronger in certain personalities than in others. People, who fully embrace life in this way in youth, continue to do so in old age.

The lesser known psychologist who also supports my theory is Prescott Lecky. In his 1945 book entitled, <u>Self Consistency, a Theory of Personality,</u> Lecky proposes that the personality is a holistic system, and "...as long as man remains alive he must be thought of as a unit in himself, a system which operates as a whole." (Lecky, 1945, 1945, P. 107) Lecky goes on to say that personality is an "organization of values" which are consistent with each other. Therefore, if a person believes in living life by fully employing and developing all his gifts and talents, he will carry that belief and act accordingly, throughout his entire lifetime.

This is not to say that the natural processes of biological aging (ie: poorer eyesight. Loss of easy retrieval from recent memory blanks, stiffness in joints, and reduced capacity of lungs to hold breath) will not take their toll on even a self actualizing person in their latter years. They however, will find a way to work around these things. They will use their creativity to become flexible and adjust circumstances to accommodate their changing bodies. They may, also, develop different gifts, more suited to their physical abilities (ie: a runner may take up painting). What they don't do, barring any major disease, is settle into a rocking chair and wait to die.

The examples in this book were taken of a man who embodies my theory: John Huckaby taken over his life from childhood, now in his 89th year, but only scrape the surface of the dynamic lifestyle that John has always lived.

Born and raised in Texas 90 years ago, John was blessed with a veritable arsenal of talents. He is a quick learner who throws himself into everything that captures his interest. He has travelled extensively: first with his father at age 13, then through the armed services and during his career as an engineer and consultant for various international companies. He retired from this work in 1986. On the side, as a "hobby" (I say this tongue in cheek) he became world famous as the "Incredible Huck" an elderly runner who competed in marathons and ultra marathons for almost 10 years before his second (not the first) heart attack convinced him to retire from the sport. The peak of his running career was 1979-1982 when he was 60 years old!

Betty, John's wife has been my landlord this year and I have seen him fix cars, do carpentry work on the apartments, write press releases (which were published), finish painting a huge mural for the United Methodist Church (a yearlong project), give excellent Godly talks at Christian workshops, give impromptu art lessons to daughter, attend art classes at California and Rome Community Art Center and Ava Dorfman Senior Center at Rome, NY, and art instructor for 10 years. His murals and paintings are worldwide. Over his lifetime, John has taught, preached, built, written, painted, run, created: owned a resort park, apartment complexes, worked as an electronic adjunct at college and military schools, and electronic communication engineer and technician around the world. The man is even an excellent cook! I wonder if there is anything he can't do. The man has been a dynamo of activity through and creativity all of his life—neither the aging process nor two heart attacks have been able to slow him down. He is, in my opinion, the best "proof" I could present of the theory that one remains self actualizing throughout his life and that old age does not have to be stagnant nor unproductive.

BIBLIOGRAPHY
Lecky, Prescott, Self-Consistency, a theory of Personality
Ft. Myers Beach, Florida: Island Press, 1945.
Maslow, Abraham, Motivation and Personality, New York:
Harper & Row, 1970 (2nd Edition).

PREFACE

The "Incredible Huck" has done it all

I am an artist and have run more than a hundred marathons and a dozen ultra marathons and survived two heart attacks, one that left me clinically dead.

They call me "The Incredible Huck." There is nothing I cannot or have not done in my life.

Let's go back to May 1983 when I lived in Rome, NY. I was running the Canadian International Marathon that May. It was there that I would have a heart attack that would leave me clinically dead. It was after this heart attack that I started painting, caressing the canvas with a brush rather than pounding the ground with my feet.

"I was bored because I could not run anymore and decided to take up painting." I then took art lessons for seventeen years and taught at Ava Dorfman Senior center for ten years, finally retiring in January 2008.

When I began painting I had no idea my paintings and murals would be seen not only in Rome NY, but state and worldwide. I credit great teachers and my background in engineering to my fame as a painter.

I have painted two best of show paintings and innumerable award winning paintings locally and afar. My first mural can be seen at the First United Methodist Church in Rome, NY.

I painted my first large 8x16 foot mural, with the help of four other artists on framed canvas. The mural is named "The Sower," a religious painting of Jesus' first parable depicting how the word of God is acted upon. The mural was completed in November 1986. This is the only mural that I had help on except once when I was helped by my teacher, Mr. Roger Morris.

I am what I call a virtuoso of drafting and have said being an engineer in my professional career has helped my art. Especially when it comes to murals, because I have no problem scaling things. My time (12 1/2 years) in 17 amphibious landings in WWII and Korea wars, as chief radio officer, and 3 years on a Greek tramp steamer as soul radio operator has helped with pictures and murals because of the things and places I have seen.

"When I was in Saudi Arabia installing a communication system for a telemetry control of oil through to 30" pipeline I had a chance to visit the Sea of Galilee and was familiar with the terrain. This gave me absolute authenticity in the mural.

When creating a painting or a large mural I use what I call my mathematical logic I learned from studying the creator of the universe. I use what I call "his trick of the trade." It is an ace in the hole. "I learned about how God built every living thing and God did so by dynamic symmetry. The Greeks used this way of thinking to create the golden age of Pericles.

I have painted a dozen large murals and twice as many smaller ones. I have also painted a set of five murals for a church in New Zealand. In addition I have painted several large theater drops for churches and schools. Photographs of my art and running feats are shown throughout this book.

Before I begin painting, I can be found in the library and museums researching my project. In one 10'x20' mural. I painted the entire book of Revelation (the last book of the bible). When creating a portrait, landscape or mural I did my research first.

The Veteran's mural and WWII and Korean War murals actually come from my heart since I am a veteran myself. I also aided the French in Vietnam. The VA mural is a 8'x7' wide illustration of the spirit of the American people. To honor those who served their country in the time of war. My WWII mural depicts the national WWII Memorial that's located between the Jefferson and Washington Memorial in Washington DC. It is located with my Korean War mural. They measure 6'x7' and 3'x4' respectively. The VA mural is located in VA conference room at the Griffith industrial and Technology Park in Rome, NY. Whereas the WWII mural is located in the Utica Center for Development Inc. for the Central NY center for Veterans at 720 Washington St, Utica, NY. The veteran's mural has three grace angels in the painting to show the kindness so deserved for the three fold assistance aiding the veterans. Each angel represents the VA Administrations specific benefits.

In my mind it was a symbol of "peace on earth" for after serving in the regular Navy for six years from 1940 to 1946 and in the suicidal amphibious attack ships Wm. P. Biddel and Harris. During WWII I had experienced over 17 landings from North Africa to Iwo Jima. I was in the landing with General Patton at Morocco and General MacArthur in Leyete Philippines and at Iwo Jima when the war ended. I am thankful for the VA over the years because they have been able to help me with home loans, provided hospital care when I was sick, and provided college education, gave me job preferences and helped me in other aspects of life.

It was a good will gesture to paint my version of the VA in the time of WWII when the American people through their legislatures founded the VA.

There is something you need to understand about me. Everything I do is 110 percent. If It is not, I do it again. I pray and seek God's advice to remain humble and avoid being proud, haughty, not arrogant, or assertive. I am a good sportsman and do me best to win fairly. Look at my running record in the age 60 and over class: On November 21-22, 1981 on a 150 meter indoor calibrated and timed track, I made a U.S. record of 101 miles, 753 yards in 24 hours, perhaps a world record that has been broken since then? I ran the Boston marathon 4 times nonstop (104.8 miles in 24 hours to protest a ruling. The standards were changed).

So to say that I paint, is an understatement. It should be, I paint incredible murals that take countless hours of research and time to paint.

For "The Incredible Huck," only perfection will do. Does I miss running? Yes, but today at age 90 with a pacemaker and defibulator to regulate my heart that was repaired by open heart surgery in 1993, art has become an integral part of my life. I have received numerous awards and recognition for my murals and paintings. My work is a representation of what I see, feel, and understand. It is the voice from my soul.

God brought me back from the edge of the grave to give him Glory through the talent He has given to me, painting.

PRESS RELEASE

JULY 1, 2007
BIRTH OF THE UTICA BOILERMAKER 15K ROAD RACE
THE UTICA BOILERMAKER HISTORY AS TAKEN FROM JOHN HUCKABY'S RUNNER LOG BOOK AND MEMORY

Sunday, July 2, 1978 at Barneveld, NY in a downtown bar after a fun run to west Canada creek, at about 9 P.M., members of the Stuben striders, Utica pacemakers and Roman runners were busy talking about the days run and about Randy Gates of the striders who had chased down a purse snatcher and bewildered the thief who didn't know he was fleeing from a marathon runner.

Earl Reed owner, operator of the Utica boiler plant sat on my right and Stuben strider Hogan sat on my left in the bar. Suddenly Earl Reed ordered a boilermaker, when served he took the shot of whisky and dumped it into the glass of beer and said, "This is a boilermaker." Then Hogan who had always had a cooler of beer and refreshments for the runners at races and fun runs, looked on in dismay and said, "I wish we had a race that ended in the back yard of a brewery so I wouldn't have to lug this heavy cooler around." Earl said, "That's a good idea. Tomorrow morning I'm going to talk with Carl Matt owner of the Utica club brewery and tell him I represent the Utica Boiler factory and a race to your brewery back yard with free beer would benefit us both." It would be good advertisemnent. An agreement was reached. On Saturday July 7, 1978 a few Stuben striders, Utica pacemakers, and Roman runners met up with Tom Hovey of the Utica pacemakers on a road near the golf course. He was riding a bicycle with a veeder root counter attached to the front tire to check the distance accurately for the 15KM (9.3 miles) race. Sunday July 9, 1978 I ran the preliminary boilermaker race as a tryout with a few others, it was 80 degrees. My weight was 145 pounds, blood pressure 130/95, and I ran the trial run in 72 minutes. The course was wonderfully designed.

Sunday July 16, 1978, the first official boilermaker foot race that was being sanctioned by the AAU(American Atheletic Union) began. It was 90 degrees, and won by a runner named Rojas who had just had a victory win up north. I ran the race in 70 minutes 36 seconds (A 7:35 pace) and got 3rd place in the 50 to 60 age category. My age was 58 and I received a nice trophy. My runner log book didn't say how many runners were in the race, but we had a good time and the beer after that hot run sure did taste good. I asked my running coach, Tom Hovey if he thought the race had a future. he said, "We tried to get elite runners here before and were unsuccessful, maybe this will change things?" What a change since that day, Sunday July 16, 1978! Isn't it amazing what can come from a bar conversation?

(note: Hogan was a nickname, the Stuben Striders can furnish his real name)
Retired Roman Runner John R. Huckaby
AKA "The Incredible Huck"

PARADISE

Got an hour?

I was asked by Carl Eilenberg to write a short article on the subject of Heaven. After my near death and out of the body experiences plus my extensive research on Paradise I felt that I could write this article. At that time I had almost completed a 10' high x 18' long mural representing three years of concept, composition and color to bring the "Book of Revelation" with all its magnificent symbols and scary prophesy into a breath taking panorama. It reveals God's final word. Depicted is the world today with wars, famine, drugs, pollution, prostitution, crime, alcoholism, murder and satan and his demons coming down out of the heavens. The planetary system shown out of orbit, the constellations disappearing in the universe. The seven headed monster, raising from the sea amongst a fleet of warships. The tribulation is shown as the world besieged by the four horsemen, the seven seals and trumpeters calling out woes resulting in angels descending to make earthquakes, storms, famine, pestilence, stinging locusts, horses with serpent tails, and the world governments in trouble. I had one angel throwing fire balls upon the Kremlin, however now that the Russian leader, Yeltsin has become a convert to the democratic system; I asked what was going to happen next? A newsman said, "The angel will probably be throwing American dollars to the Russians." Coming out of a cave is the two headed beast with symbol 666 of the world empire of false religion. Included is the woman standing on the moon with the baby in her arms signifying the birth of God's kingdom. The spiritual battle of Armageddon and the resurrection of the dead who join forces with the ones living through the tribulation who won't experience death are shown marching up to the top of Mount Zion. The final phase and last third of the painting depicts God on his throne surrounded by the four living creatures with a hall of green jasper in the background. Christ has a long steel rod in his hand to rule as a king and not as a Christmas baby. The Holy Spirit rounds out the trio with the form of a grayish dove. Then the most beautiful scene conceivable: Paradise itself. The New Jerusalem, coming down from the Heavens. It was fifteen hundred square miles; it had a wall about 212 feet high around it with twelve pearly gates and an angel at each gate with the inscription of the twelve apostles and the twelve tribes of Israel over and under each gate. I really enjoyed researching and painting the foundation of God's kingdom. It took me several months to research and paint the foundation. The first stone was precious Jasper. It is found in the Rocky Mountains however a very rare and beautiful stone of Jasper is located in India and Sri Lanka. Some types are greenish and others an orangish tone with landscape designs embedded in them. The other stones were gems as follows: sapphire, chalcedony, emerald, sardonyx, sardius, chrysolite, beryl, topaz, chrysoprase, hyacinth, and amethyst. I ground rocks and used gold leaf to add to the pigments to paint these gems. Flowing from the New Jerusalem, the kingdom of God, flowing from the center was a river of the water of life, clear as a crystal flowing out from the throne of God. On each side of the river were trees producing twelve crops of fruit (one for each month). The power of God generated the light in brilliant silvery streamers. I painted the tree of life just like a cherry tree in blossom in the spring time. To those who wish to take life's water free, I showed them in my painting tugging, pulling and leading loved ones to the water's edge so they could drink their fill by cupped hands or large buckets, all nationalities I put in Paradise, they are picking apples, grapes oranges and bananas from fruit trees. However, there was work there, I didn't paint anyone goofing off, no Beetle Baileys. After completing the book of Revelation, I had a left over area three foot high and six foot long. I checked for other information on Paradise, and I found in book of Isaiah 11:6, the Lion would muzzle the calf, the wolf would lie down with the sheep, the leopard be with the kid (goat) and a little boy would lead them. So I used my grandsons as models for this. These scriptures were added to the ones from Revelation.

The most gratifying part of the painting was St. Michael (Christ) warring with Satan and Satan being thrown into the lake of fire. To date my mural is completed.

My wife Betty thinks that our small French Poodle named Pierre-Louiee, will be there in Paradise to greet her by wagging his little tail. From what I've experienced in several near death experiences, Paradise appeared to me as an abstract, sort of fuzzy place, a twofold kingdom of earth and sky. The earth will be a new earth like the one that Adam and Eve lived in, a real Paradise. The very thought of missing out on that scares me into virtue along with thoughts of the alternate route. For me, I don't think death is the end of a miserable journey. From my visions and the things seen, the end is worth what is coming. Happiness is so short lived, if you have something worthwhile today, tomorrow comes the fear of losing it. When I grow older, no one is going to turn back the years. Actually most people don't want to hear about Heaven and Paradise, but life on this earth now is finite (limited). I sometimes get tired of constant Joy. However, I have faith that what we have here is not all, my faith is soundly based on the fact yes, Virginia, "There is a God" and he has revealed Himself to me personally and through my eyes as an artist I find using his dimensions of life in every painting. The scriptural definition of faith in Hebrews 11:1 can be illustrated as follows: The little girl's mother tells or promises her if she cleans up her room her mother will take the little girl to get an ice cream cone. As the little girt proceeds to clean up her room there is no doubt the promise will be kept. As an artist painter, I prefer visual things, don't tell me about it, and show me, now. The thing that we fear most about Paradise is we have to die to get there unless we go thru the tribulation. Just think the last judgment. Are we lucky. When God forgives, he forgets and gives us a clean sheet. After my latest near death experience, I try to be more faithful to my duties. My faith being like a saran wrap shield, I strain to see through it to see where I'm at and where I'm going. Paradise appears to me as both a place and a state of mind. In my first near death experience I tried to run towards God who was setting in judgment but my feet seemed stuck in mud and life passed before me, no flesh has seen God and lived, only in spirit like astral projection, I don't think Christ's body was taken to heaven, God disposed of it somehow, even when returning Christ took on several different bodies. For example, on the road to Emmaus, confronting the doubting Thomas, eating fish with Simon Peter and the day of Pentecost. In some of my near death experiences my vision appeared blurred, out of focus, like an imperfect optical lens, it was a hellish experience. It is through love alone that much of God's creation is presented to me for enjoyment, at its best I can only copy what exists in the world, the flowers, landscapes, the lakes and good things to eat; the eternal cycle of the seasons must have an author. The skies with all their amazing wonders and vastness, what laws confound the atheist. The God of Abraham and his creative ability alone created Paradise and is in full command of the ultimate direction of this universe. Paradise starts right here on this earth, the bible is absolutely God's book. No precious word of truth I received in my fourth vision was "If you think right you will act right" actions follows thoughts, I cannot think evil thoughts and act like a saint.

I believe there will be an all out spiritual war and Satan and his demons will be relegated to the fiery pit and suffer along with any who blasphemes the Holy Spirit. Any other rejects will simply be zapped out of creation. The tent of God is with mankind, He has promised us we won't be discouraged, tired, mentally drained, there will be no starvation, no more tears, pain, death, tragedy, outcry or disappointment, no grief, no sorrow and mourning, they are gone.

How amazing to see a place where there is everlasting ecstatic joy. Living on this earth is the beginning of life in Heaven, Paradise, or Hell. To permanently get to one place or the other, we must die or live through the great tribulation when it arrives. In Paradise, think of the joy of seeing your friends and relatives, this would contribute to their ultimate joy. Helen Keller, born blind and deaf will be astounded to hear God's voice and see all the beautiful things to be had in Paradise. Just think she never saw a flower, tree, ocean wave or heard music (some of it today she's just as well off).

There will be two types of people in Paradise. The ones that have suffered much the deprived, crippled ones, born losers and the ones who were more fortunate in life and did God's will. The Heavens will find the kingdom with the angels, living creatures, God, his son Jesus Christ, and the 24 elders: these will be the Heavenly organization to establish and carry out the management of Paradise, the new earth. There will be no bad memories, no guilt, bad dreams, experiences, sorrows, regrets, no ups and downs. Something always to be joyful and happy about, joy starts right here on this earth. A receipt for cherry pie is not the same as eating the cherry pie. Faith plays a major role in God's answer, prayers or even having them. Joy is the sign of God's presence living or even being with us. Joy can disappear when just one person can't stand us. Even the will of God figures in just how much joy we will have now and hereafter. Repenting is a difficult thing to do, it means doing an about face.

I was curious about work in Paradise, my first thoughts were "I worked all my life, and don't want to work in Paradise." But on second thought "A place of happiness can't be idleness." Even spiritual muscles disintegrate; there is much work in Paradise. God worked for six days to make this earth. God is not a zombie. Just to plan creation took a lot of work, sometimes however, little details appear to have slipped through, like the long neck of the giraffe. It must have been a lot of fun. Can't we take out all the fun when we try to explain many things? Before Christ cured the sick he cleaned up their spiritual beings like "go and sin no more" or "your sins are forgiven." I don't think anyone will be selling in paradise. There will be no fatigue, not even for intellectual, the hardest kind of work. All our scientific data is like a tiny island in a large sea of the unknown, as we learn the more our shoreline grows. The more you learn the more there is to learn; look at the scientific discoveries in the last 50 years. You have to be gentle when you don't feel so, if you don't think that works, you haven't worked! You will have to do a lot of praying for your friends, families and loved ones on earth; that should take up a lot of your time. Spiritual work is never finished. We all must rise above the mundane.

One of my visions of Paradise was truly unique. I saw a hill over looking a verdant plain green as an emerald like a jasper stone, the sky cerulean bluish hue in profound chroma and ultimate in intensity, filled with snow white cumulous clouds like marshmallows. The pathways were lined and divided by garden flowers, unlike any flower I ever saw, I've tried to paint them in my mural of the heavens. They resembled orchids. Exquisite trees of pink and gold inlaid with emerald greens. Their trunks studded with glittering diamonds. Building of such beauty and magnificent in shape, nothing could compare. Then I heard music, the harps, thermions, vibrant violins with harmoning vibrettos. The music sounded like hundreds of symphonic instruments, there was no rap to be heard, no slang no perverse innuendos. All the people are enjoying themselves, some playing, and some talking. I recognized my father and Bill Coughlin, father was walking and Bill was running, I could have reached out and touched them both. Father had a tunic of diamonds and a sash of garnets. Happiness, we must have the light of glory, no lights are comparable; playing and loving is the greatest work of all.

I found Paradise to be an extension of our present life, our companionship in Paradise may be with great minds, and we will know the great whys. Looking about I tried to find someone I knew who was not there, and wondered why sometimes we love some one person today and hate them later? Today families seem torn to shreds, how strange to love as God loves. I noticed that God has enemies in Heaven and in Paradise on earth, I came to the conclusion that He even loved Satan but was at odds with his slanderous and evil and opposing ways. Most people looked to be about 33 years old in Paradise. There were people who had resulted from abortions, miscarriages and even people who had been eaten by lions. Paradise is a place where you see those you loved and didn't love. This earth is not all that God made. The sunrise, sunset, a rainbow, the power of the wind, the sun peeking through the clouds; do you think that's it? Nothing like it is that which is to come. All our suffering and pain are gone, the kingdom halls and meadows of Paradise are filled with love.

Through prayer a spring of life rises in the heart, from that spring comes grace (God's underserved kindness) and is like music beautiful to all, like the sounds of nature, the breeze, rustling leaves, silence and leaves crackling underfoot. A water fall, an ocean wave, quiet but poweful, but life thoughts shut them out, all the beauty that a solemn stillness holds. What God hears isn't what we feel; hit an empty vessel with a fork and the sound is phenomenal. That sound pierces to Paradise. Music of the heart can't be expressed in words. The heart speaks and sings; love is a song, a melody, very content and happy for a few hours, take a walk or a trip and your joyness is a different kind of music not like the notes on a scale. Music of light that shines on the soul, the smile on the face of a child, music of accomplishment, work well done, when sinners repent the angles sing. Music of friendship, hearts bulging.

In Paradise memories are restored. I didn't just sit around and say holy, holy, holy. It seemed to be a continuous study, learning the whys and how's of the creation. The Creator was teaching his truth and laws. The lack of knowledge today is our major problem. It is our ignorance that often leads us into hell. My largest problem being, "I didn't really know myself." In Paradise our imperfections and limitations are gone! On earth we didn't know exactly what we were doing. Higher prayer in the kingdom of God was easy to obtain. Earthly human nature always leaves us with doubts and misunderstandings. Thoughtless. The will of God here is too remote. People do not like other people's tastes in clothing, cars or even ties. On this old earth I never quite arrived at self knowledge, or humbleness. Always living in fear, past, present and future. Guilt, I kept bringing it back. That mask was discarded in Paradise. The struggle is gone in Paradise, no more fighting to be good, gentle, not impatient, no moral problems, the great reward, the coveted prize. God is truly the bright and shining light in the darkness. In fact He will generate the light when the sun and moon are passed away. On earth now, things seem to go from bad to worse. In Paradise, we will understand. There will be no end to the things we understand. Angels will share their knowledge. The friend I despised may be much higher in the kingdom. All mysteries of the scriptures are opened. Which one caused us to change the book of Revelation will unfold. God's spirit will give us knowledge and perfection.

We influence people every day. Today many parents are heartsick over their children. Sometimes God brings us down, tragedy, remember God is here to bear us up on eagle wings. Why are most sermons on hell and so few on Paradise? One specialist who had studied for years about eyes said, "I know so very little," there is no boredom in Paradise. God's love kept us busy learning about love and for time indefinite.

Reading about out of body experiences and near death experiences does not do much to cause people to repent. Faith comes by hearing, and hearing by the word of God. Remember the rich man in Hell asked Lazarus to go back to his father's house and testify to 5 brothers lest they also come into this place of torment. Abraham said "they had

Moses and the prophets, let them hear them," he said, "nay but if one from the dead went to them, they would repent." He said "if they didn't hear Moses and the prophets, they wouldn't be persuaded by one of the dead." All of us who have had near death experiences will someday die and when that occurs we will be conscious of nothing. "The soul that is sinning in itself will die." The soul does not survive the death of the body with which living humans can thereafter communicate. God has your soul information recorded somehow; the thing that returns to God is his spirit force which you have been using while alive. Time does not have meaning to one dead, just like a deep sleep, the whole night can zip by and if you didn't dream, it seems instantaneous. "Or ever the silver cord be loosed, then shall the dust return to the earth as it was: and the spirit shall return unto God who gave it." (Ecclesiastes 12:6.7)

If a man die, shall he live again? asked the man Job so long ago. Your dead ones will live and rise up and the good will have the earth and live on it forever. In the beginning Adam and Eve died because they disobeyed God's instructions and they returned to the ground. Sin brings death but God gives everlasting life. When a person dies, he or she goes back to the ground but their spirit goes out, his thoughts perish. We inherit sin and death from Adam. You are a soul, and the soul that sins die. The dead will be restored to life by a resurrection. To God everyone lives. Christ said the hour will come when the dead shall rise at the sound of God's voice. Christ ordered the dead man at Nain to "Get up" and he raised Jairus's daughter, and Lazarus who was dead for four days. Have confidence in the resurrection draw close to God and he will sustain you. The fear of God is the beginning of wisdom. In Paradise people and animals will live in peace. God will satisfy all needs and desires of all living things on the new earth under the Kingdom management. This concept is hard to understand because today man is unable to rule himself, conditions are getting worse, there are: food shortages, great earthquakes, lawlessness, loss of love, anguish of nations, critical times: hard to deal with, we must realize that God's kingdom is at hand. At this very moment everlasting life depends upon taking in knowledge of the true God of Abraham and his son Jesus Christ. Satan is the invisible power that controls the nations of the world. Today's wars uses fearful gases, napalm, atomic and nuclear bombs, flame throwers, concentration camps, mass murder of millions. Over 200,000,000 have died by wars since world war 1. Satan is a real spirit person who chose his course of action which made him a slanderer, oppose, liar. The devil is not a creature with horns and a pitchfork, who oversees some underground place of torment. He is really a powerful but wicked angel. He says, "People don't need God."

After telling a lady about my near death experiences she said, "Your stories give me goose bumps." At age 16 I had two brief encounters with death. The first being when the malaria fever ran into black jaundice. While undergoing x-ray treatment of the spleen, I lapsed into a coma and felt my body slipping away. The farce was ending and I was seeking a great perhaps. The x-ray machine was used to drive the malaria sporozoan parasites in the red blood cells out of the spleen so the quinine drug could destroy them. My heart stopped and for a while, I was suspended over my body by a silver cord. I remember the technician shouting "he's gone" and my father trying to pull me back. When I went back into my body my eyes opened and there was the technician, my father and mother and the fat doctor smoking a corked cigar. My father had sold my pet calf for $28 to pay the hospital bill there in Oklahoma.

My next encounter with out of the body experiences with death came during my senior year in high school. I was playing center on the school football team. We played the Anadarko Indians. I remember centering the football when the Choctaw Indian hit me and then there were stars, I hovered over my body and they hauled me away on a stretcher. Again the silver cord kept me earthbound. We lost the game six to nothing.

There were other times when I collapsed from loss of blood or passed out from double pneumonia. The most unforgettable out of body experience was in Ottawa, Canada on May 15, 1983. It was my 130th marathon. Nearing the 26 mile mark on Carlton College I collapsed and fell into a ditch. Two nurses just happened to be driving past and saw me laying in the ditch. They gave me CPR as my heart was not beating and my breathing had stopped. I was clinically dead. An ambulance with two paramedics and a doctor just happened by and they happened to have a 10,000 volt defribulator with them. They zapped me with it twice and I jumped up and tried to continue running the marathon. Again I was attached to my body by a silver cord which momentarily snapped, it was then strange things took place. The most beautiful music and lights of every color flashed. I received a message from the unknown, you are going back, you must do something in return. You must paint murals of God's scriptures in the bible. Suddenly the silver cord was attached to my head and it was pulling me back to my body, which was being rushed to the Ottawa General Hospital. Upon entering my body, I awoke and there were half a dozen nurses in pink uniforms. If they had been white, I'd have known I'd made it. That night in the intensive care ward I received the gift of art for God. The next morning looking out the window I beheld a landscape and drew it. Before this I had sketched my enginerring projects and given them to my draftsman. Now suddenly I could draw and latter paint the images that God set before me.

My latest near death experience that resulted in an out of body experience was in Albany Medical Center on August 9, 1993. During open heart bypass surgery, near the end when angioplasty surgery failed for the fifth time, my heart stopped. I remember the doctors working over me and my wife looking at the TV monitor, then the cord snapped but as I seemed to be hurled into infinite space an angel appeared. They had an oxygen tube down my throat so I couldn't speak. I remember using deaf sign languages with my hands. The angel said, "it was the prayers of my wife that saved me." Betty has always been very good and helpful with her prayers. Once she said, "All I can do is pray," I said, "that's like having two guardian angels."

Paradise- The garden of Eden itself, or the earth as a whole when it will be transformed in the future to a condition like that of Eden, or flourishing spiritual conditions among God's servants on earth, or provisions in heaven that remind one of Eden.

Heaven- The dwelling place of the God of Abraham. Also the dwelling place of faithful spirit creatures. It is a realm invisible to human eyes. Also represents God's organization of faithful spirit creatures, a position of divine favor, the physical universe apart from the earth, the expanse surrounding planet earth, no human governments under Satan's domination, and the righteous new heavenly government in which Jesus Christ with his joint heirs are empowered by God to rule.

Kingdom- The kingdom of God is the expression of God's universal sovereignty towards his creatures, or the means used by Him to express that sovereignty through the royal government headed by his Son Jesus Christ. "Kingdom" may refer to the rulership of the one anointed as King or to the earthly realm ruled by that heavenly government.

Book One

CHAPTER 1

THE HUCKABYS SINCE 1764

In the Huckaby Registry, Early Huckaby Immigranted to North America. The individuals who left their homes for life in the New World were undoubtedly courageous. Research through reference books containing ship passenger lists, led me to the discovery of the first two immigrants. Peter Wilson listing of: English Convicts in Colonial America, lists William Huckaby arriving in the New World in 1764. Michell Lois Dumas, Mobil Ship News: Mobile, Alabama lists: First name not available—Huckaby arrived in Mobile, Alabama in 1822 with wife and daughter. Little information is available on William, as to why he was sent to a prison camp in New Orleans, La. The story goes, that after several years he escaped from busting rocks and ran to Texas.

Ralph Waldo Emerson wrote: "We are the children of many sires, and every drop of blood in us in its turn betrays its ancestor."

My grandfather, Samuel Huckaby fought in the Civil War and was with Robert E. Lee in several battles. Once, he was struck by a mini ball in his forehead but survived. When he came home, his wife saw him with a foot long beard and went "bananas." My father, Robert Gould Huckaby, was born April 8, 1890. My Dad never saw his mother. At his birth his mother Lucy was admitted to a mental institution in Austin, Texas. Dad was nursed by a black woman he called Aunt Lucy and she raised him along with her own baby. When Dad was five years of age, he fell off a wagon loaded with oak logs and it ran over his legs and broke them both. It was then that his education began. The only thing for him to study was a large illustrated dictionary. So by the time he could walk again, he became a walking dictionary.

My father was truly an amazing self actualization man. He could draw, paint and sculpture on par with the best artists. Another gift, his cabinet making ability, was profound. He became a petroleum engineer by completing an advanced course in geology and could find oil using an old apple branch. He was also a lapidary. He could cut fine stones and make beautiful jewelry.

After attending an old country school, he continued operating the family farm at Edge, Texas. He then left to see the world. He went to Louisiana and took a job as a Zinc smelter. The temperature rose to the point that he thought he was in hell. On his way back to Texas my father bought a magazine, only to discover a list of lovelorn single girls. My father wrote a letter to a young lady named Stella that later became my mother. He was 24 when the love bug hit him.

Dad rode his horse named "Starlight" over two hundred miles to a small Texas town named "Eldorado" (Spanish for City of Gold). When he arrived at the very large farm, he was met by mom's three wild cowboy brothers. They decided to shoot him or hang him from a mesquite tree. However, after hearing him talk, they decided that instead of shooting him or hanging him that this is the right guy to manage the 2,000 acre farm and ranch. Dad took the job, married their sister and worked with their father to run the property. A short time afterwards they were called to fight in WWI and sent to France. My father was found physically unfit to go to battle due to flat feet or something, so was left behind with Stella. John's sister Edna was born in 1916 and had a thyroid disorder that she had her entire life. John helped her and graduated from high school.

When two of Stella's brothers returned from war, (brother Earl was killed in the war), my father, mother and sister left for Ranger, Tx since oil had been struck there. Dad caught typhoid fever and almost died but by the grace of God he survived and took a petroleum engineering job with the P&G Oil Company. He was put in charge of 35 each 55,000 barrel oil tanks. The property was posted so we were isolated and us kids had to walk over a mile to school. Lightening hit a tank, to shoot holes in tank to let oil in dyke to burn. Dad had used a Civil War Cannon.

A miracle in its self, I, John Robert was born on his father's birthday, April 8, 1921. My father thought it was a supernatural work of God. As a young boy, I would chase swift long legged birds called "road runners," coyotes (small wolf), sage hens and jack rabbits. My legs became stronger than a bionic child. My father said I could run "like the wind." This was a big advantage because it gave me the ability to outrun the big mean kids.

In the first grade, my artistic ability and creativity took place. The larger boys gave me pennies to tell stories from my imagination and draw funny animals in action. They liked my story about the farmer and his kicking donkey. The schools in 1926 taught reading, writing, arithmetic, and God, Jesus and the Holy Spirit. Along with the bible and patriotic songs.

My father told me, "Son if you don't believe there's a God you damn sure better believe there's a devil." He went on to say "there are a wide variety of cultural and religious practices to fill our need for spirituality, but the bible gives a clear answer." My father believed in Purposeful Design rather than mindless process. He was thoroughly convinced in a creator and intelligent design. "That everything God made had a purpose except the mosquito that gave us both the malaria fever."

One day at the age of six while I was with my father dumping the trash, I found a magnet in the dump. I was truly amazed that it would pick up tin cans. It was at that time I made the discoverery of magnetism. This was my first discovery in electronics that eventually lead me on a lifelong career.

At the age of eight I built my first radio set. My father enjoyed it so much that I made another one for myself along with a transmitter so I could become a ham radio operator. I was sending messages by Morse code and had an all out obsession. Instead of just reading my school books, I was fully engrossed in: electronics and communication theory. So when I was just ten years old, I would repair all the neighbors' radios as they became inoperative.

During all this time my other gift or talent took form. I began to sculpt wood and soap into people, animals and other objects. Also, I started to paint many pictures of landscapes, objects and people. In addition to my school education, I resorted to reading and studing the twenty volume set of encyclopedias. I wanted to read and study them so I could acquaint myself with all the world wonders of that era. Science had not advanced but was just the beginning of man making full use of all his creative knowledge, and extending it through astounding inventions. During my childhood Dad drove a Model T Ford that he started with a hand operated crank. Mom did the laundry using a rub board in the wash and bath tub. The ice man put ice in our refrigerator. I did homework by candle light. The radio was in its infancy and air travel was unknown. Medical treatment was very limited and television, computers, internet, cell phones, neon lights, etc. had not even been invented yet. What man has created, invented, manufactured, bought and sold in the last 100 years would fill a library of books. Sometimes even the inventions have lead to greater things such as putting a man on the moon, nuclear weapons and reactors, super highways throughout the nation, modern trains, cars and busses, cellphones and computers. The list goes on and on. The devil has been active. God, Jesus and all other religions barred from our school and other public places since 1962. No doubt our founding fathers are turning in their graves.

I made a retort to make gasoline from crude oil for the family car. I made alcohol out of corn but my father destroyed it before the revenuers discovered it.

My father, Robert Gould Huckaby was named after a wealthy man named, J. Gould. My mother Stella Booth, was a descendant of the founder of the Salvation Army in England. She was a very charitable woman who never failed to give soup to the hungry at the door. My sister Edna was born in 1916 with a Thyroid disorder. She was over four years older than myself; however I took care of her and helped her through high school.

Edna was also a diabetic; she died at the age of 50 from a diabetes mellitus attack in the back seat of a sheriff's car a few minutes prior to reaching the hospital at San Angelo Texas. The rush to save her life was inhibited by the frantic fifty mile trip. She was barren and had no children. It was a blessing as she married an ex-convict that abandoned her. She went to live with our mother at Eldorado, Tx. until her death in 1966.

My brother Basil was born in 1925 and graduated from high school just in time to enter WWII. Talk about self actualization, Basil served in the Navy aboard the USS Salt Lake City. A heavy cruiser that fought in most sea battles in the Pacific. During the Aleutian Island campaign he fed the shells into the eight inch guns firing at the Japanese fleet. A Jap shell hit his turret and he was sent to a hospital in Waco, Texas. After five years he escaped and fled to San Angelo, Texas. He took a job in a gas station changing tires until he got enough money to buy it. He bought land and invested his money wisely. Today he is a multi-millionaire. The last account of Basil he had 18, 1955 Chevrolet autos in the back yard of his homestead and a rich wife and an oil lease. Basil bought some city lots at give away prices and later a thruway was built through them. He did so much for our country and God is repaying him.

John's Homestead, Farm and oilwell marker Eldorado, Tx
Problems caused two wells to be drilled 15' outside farm
Gushers still pumped, 1980

CHAPTER 2

AGE 12 TO 19 (YOUTH TO NAVY ENLISTMENT)

When I was age 12, my father was transferred from Ranger, Tx to Gorman, Tx and I entered school there in the sixth grade. It was the 1933 and the depression was at it's worst. We had to eat jam sandwiches (two pieces of bread, biscuits jammed together). My memory strangely reached a higher level and I was able to recite poems, stage act and recall data from all my classes and from my set of encyclopedias, plus I became a whiz at mathematics. My avid thirst for knowledge and action developed me into a bookworm, carpenter, electrician, actor, mason, organic/inorganic chemist, watch repair, household appliances repair, radio, telephone, auto malfunctions, I became Mr. Fix it. I was also a sportsman. Shooting rabbits, birds, squirrels and any other small animals was distasteful. They were so pretty and had a Godful purpose, why not paint them or draw them? I was content with knocking the tin cans off a fence post with my BB gun. My father could shoot from his hip and knock all the cans off. When I was in Navy boot camp on the 200 yard rifle target range, I missed being an expert rifleman by one shot that he wasted on another man's target. My problem was being near sighted. I would lean over the gun stock so as to use my left eye. When the high powered old 30-06 fired and recoiled, the stock would smash into my nose. I always ended up with a bloody nose and lost the extra $2.00 a month reward.

At this period in time I went through a transformation in my life. My father had an old leather covered bible with pictures and torn pages that were yellow from use and age. I started reading it and learning the whole story of creation, the existence of God, his son Jesus and salvation by faith and not by sight. I found the story of Creation in Genesis to be logical, everything just as written: every time God spoke things came into existence in the proper order (water, land, light, food, clothing, shelter, and safety and love before making Adam and Eve). I was fully knowledgeable of atoms, electrons, protons, neutrons and molecules plus electromagnetic waves. I had a listing of the 72 known elements of that time. I knew a diamond was pure carbon made under extreme heat and pressure, so God was a very strong spirit! I concluded "the disembodiment of a dead person sometimes can leave the unseen world and appear to the living in bodily likeness!" Eg. Occasionally the ghost like soldiers killed in Civil War can be seen marching.

In 1935 my family was being moved to Crane Texas. Oil was sold from the Sinclair oil co storage tanks at Gorman and Desdemona Texas. We lived 12 miles out on a tank farm that was located on the McElRoy ranch. It was within a posted area that had 30+ tanks. The school bus could come no closer than six miles from our home therefore Dad and Mom drove us to the transport connect.

This was a true God send. Now I had unlimited space to build several directional antenna's that was needed for radiating and receiving radio waves. Today it is referred to as a rhombic antenna with unidirectional transceiver capability of radio waves. I was overwhelmed with joy. It was possible to contact ham radio men and women from all parts of the world.

In the year 1936, the ranch foreman gave me a quarter horse to help round up the hundreds of Hereford cattle. They were red with white faces. Once my Jersey cow escaped from the barn and joined the herd but I lassoed the cow and put her back. Then I milked bossey who gave us milk, butter and cheese. Dad bought the family an Electrolux fridge that was run by a candle.

My art progressed at an unbelievable speed and quality, especially my sculpting talent. In my freshman year in high school in a Texas State championship carving contest, I made a streamlined cat out of a bar of soap and won second place. This put my self actualization in high gear. I started running, playing soccer, Jr. football, wrestling, drawing and painting portraits, plus gaining a sound anatomy understanding.

The early and mid 1930's were an exciting era. Popeye, Annie, Barney Google, Jack Benny, Walt Disney, Amelia Earhart, Lindbergh, FDR, Hitler, Mussolini, Floyd, Dillinger, Kelly, Churchill, Garland, Roonie, Fields and a host of western actors along with Flash Gordon and the all time great movie actors. I could see a good movie for a dime and play the pinball machine for a penny. I was much more interested in building soap cars, go cars using washing machine engines at age 16. January 1937 the oil was sold and the family moved to Ringling, Oklahoma. My father was put in charge of twenty 80,000 barrel oil tanks. My sister Edna and I went to Zanies high school while my brother Basil went to Ringling grade school. It was an explosion of learning for me as I learned to play several musical instruments including the guitar, harmonica, banjo and a one string violin and also the ukulele. I made a real violin, carved the wood, molded sides in mom's pressure cooker, etc. My father could really play that violin well. Strangely I took a great interest in algebra, geometry, trigonometry, biology, chemistry, geography, physics, and music and even more in art and sports.

JOHN CENTERS THE BALL 1936
ZANIES HIGH SCHOOL
OKLAHOMA

In 1938 I started to play on the football team as center line. Well that was a bad choice because as soon as the ball was snapped, the quarterback ran over me and the opposing team ran over my back with cleated shoes. In those days in Oklahoma it was a very rough sport. In our league we played with the fierce Anadarko Indians. Their pep squad girls would come out at half time and wave tomahawks and give war hoops. We lost the championship to them and the Wilson, Ok team 6-0. I was lettered and got a red football jacket with a big black "Z" on it. I had great success in the art field during the last of the high school years. I won first prize in the state regional contest for my graphic painting and my stage acting performance in a show named "Smokescreen" where I played the part of a drug addict, disguised as such to trick the killer into telling where the gun was hidden. Another discovery I made was that I could run very long distances with little or no effort. So in the evenings before dark I would run and run and run.

Upon graduation from high school I started my own business. I would carve figurative objects in bold relief, make a mold, and cast them in artificial marble. Then paint them and sell them to the public and novelty stores. In addition I had a full time radio repair business making a fair salary. I continued to run my small business until my patriotism urged him to join the Navy. On June 10, 1940 I enlisted for duty. As I now remember, four days later in boot camp during bayonet practice the old chief announced that France had fallen to Hitler. From that day forward I went through all the years in which included the entire WWII and Korean conflict and running weapons to Viet Nam.

Book Two

CHAPTER 3

US NAVY JUNE 14, 1940 TO JUNE 14, 1946

Boot camp was located in San Diego, California. We won the pennant for having the best marching company. My music training helped me as it was easy to keep in step with the drummer leading us. One time while marching and not paying attention, my head bobbled and they put me in charge of the Head (a ships toilet). A toilet was plugged up and the captain saw me cleaning it out with my hand. He gave us the coveted award, the barrack pennant for a whole month. That put me in good standing with the company commander.

At the completion of basic training they gave me a typing test to see what my qualification for a specific duty would be. My score was 100% for 25 WPM with no errors. Checking my civilian record they placed me in Radio Communication School, which was just my luck. Being able to take Morse code at 25 WPM on a typewriter as a ham radio operator and transmit the code at 15 WPM made life easy and avoided the cleaning detail.

A two week leave of absence (furlough) over Christmas 1940 to go back home was thrilling. We located a lady who had bought a new car and we three radiomen each gave her $30.00 to take us to Dallas, Tx. She drove to El Passo, Tx and the sailor named Loop took over driving the car. He was driving around 85 mph when just leaving the city of Midland, Tx on a sharp curve, going around a car he hit an oncoming car head on. He was killed instantly, the lady's head broke the windshield, the two men next to me had numerous bruises and my lower teeth went through my lower lip. They rushed me to the hospital where the doctor sewed me up with a, dozen or so stitches. Christmas day 1940, when getting home my mother had a big dinner for me. But I couldn't eat anything except soup through a straw. It was then that my thoughts turned to God our creator and thanked Him.

President Roosevelt was meeting Winston Churchill and agreed that we would occupy Iceland and release the British soldiers so they could return to England and defend their country. We were successful; however one of our radiomen went AWOL and married one of the blond Danish girls that we had picked up on our second trip delivering Army troops. On our second trip, a German torpedo just missed our ship and hit the escort destroyer, Rubbin James, another sank the Kearney, in the spring of 1941.

BATTLE OF MIDWAY DETAIL FROM VA MURAL
SIZE: 8" x 10 ½"
ARTIST: JOHN R. HUCKABY
LOCATED: VA SVC. CENTER
GRIFFITH BUSINESS & TEC,
PARK, ROME, NY.

GENERAL PATTON
DETAIL FROM VA MURAL
SIZE: 8" x 10½" OIL
ARTIST: JOHN R. HUCKABY
LOCATED: VA SVC. CENTER
GRIFFITH BUSINESS & TECH.
PARK, ROME, NY.

WWII PRESIDENT & GENERALS
DETAIL FORM VA MURAL
SIZE: 8" x 10½" OIL
LOCATED: VA SVC. CENTER
GRIFFITH BUSINESS & TECH.
PARK, ROME, NY.

ADMIRALS KING AND NIMITZ
DETAIL FROM VA MURAL
SIZE: 8" 10½" OIL
ARTIST: JOHN R. HUCKABY
LOCATED: VA SVC, CENTER
GRIFFITH BUSINESS & TEC
PARK, ROME, NY.

ADMIRAL HALSEY
DETAIL FROM VA MURAL
SIZE: 8" X 10 ½" OIL
ARTIST: JOHN R, HUCKABY
LOCATION: VA SVC. CENTER
GRIFFITH BUSINESS & TECH.
PARK, ROME, NY.

ADMIRALS FLETCHER & SPRUANCE
DETAIL FROM VA MURAL
SIZE: 8" 10 ½" OIL
ARTIST: JOHN R. HUCKABY
LOCATED VA SVC. CENTER
GRIFFITH BUSINESS & TEC.
PARK, ROME NY.

Upon graduating from radio school, I was transferred to the troop transport ship USS Wm. P. Biddle. We left San Diego, Ca with over 2,000 of the 6th Marines and rendezvoused near Nova Scotia. Hitter's army had driven the British army out of France with the defeat at Dunkirk. The attack transport ship Biddle sailed for Iceland. President Roosevelt and Sir Winston Churchill came to an agreement that American Marines and Army personnel would occupy Iceland so that the British troops could return to England. We stayed there about a week and then set sail for Reykiavik, Iceland. America wasn't officially at war with Germany, but they hit our escort ships, the Kearney and the Rubin James, with torpedoes causing one of them to sink. There were German u-boats everywhere. The flag command contrans 013 was aboard the Biddle. After unloading the 6th Marines, we proceeded back to New York City and picked up two thousand Army personnel to relieve the Marines. (All the Marines had polar bear emblems on their uniforms) For this, we received a letter "A" in our Atlantic Liberation Medal Ribbon. While we were loading up at the New York City 57th street of embarkation, the Yankees and the Brooklyn Dodgers were playing a game in the 1941 World Series. The game was over when the catcher dropped the ball and lost the game. We four RM3x radiomen received orders to report to Seattle Washington and go abroad the newly commissioned transport ship, the U.S.S. Harris APA-2. This was a sister ship to APA-1, the Zeilen. We left for San Diego.

It was then that WWII began in a surprise attack on Pearl Harbor. The attack came suddenly and that's just what the Japanese had intended it to be. My heart sank and a certain fear entered my thought. We were in the San Diego harbor and I was talking to our captain when a messenger scurried over and handed the captain an urgent message which read "Japanese planes attack Pearl Harbor, this is no drill." That night as we listened to the radio broadcast from President Franklyn D Roosevelt, he declared war on Japan and Germany.

We formed a convoy and with an aircraft carrier we headed toward Pearl Harbor. Seventy-two hours before reaching Honolulu, the aircraft carrier was torpedoed and went into dry dock. We reached Pearl Harbor on Christmas day in 1941 and received the shock of our lives. Four battleships were sunk and four were damaged. The minelayer and target ship was sunk. Three light cruisers, three destroyers a seaplane tender, repair ship were damaged. Two hundred and nineteen planes, several flights of B-17 bombers as the attack began. All of this was the result of three hundred and fifty Japanese aircraft.

The two man Japanese submarines were destroyed. Everything was burned. Then our mission was to evacuate the dependents of the military personnel. The U.S.S. Harris made two trips and took over four thousand dependents back to San Diego. Colonel and Doolittle planes took off from the U.S.S. Enterprise on April 18, 1942 and bombed Tokyo. With the last load of dependents, some sailors named Hebrew, Moon and Brupt fermented some of the load of pineapple juice in breakers and got some of the seedier girls drunk. They were caught and at the court martial the Captain asked, "Which one of you was a professional bootlegger on the outside?"

Our first invasion came in the summer of 1942 when the landing of troops on Wallis Island, about two hundred miles west of Samoa. We trained on North Island in San Diego and I had been promoted to RM3C. I carried a TBY transceiver on my back, a five meter rig. One of the LCVP 50 landing boats capsized upside down in the rough surf. Lt. Cruz drowned; my SOS saved the lives of others. I received a Meritorious Award.

The American Navy lucked out as no aircraft carriers were at Pearl Harbor. The aircraft Saratoga was with the Harris in San Diego harbor when the raid on Pearl knocked out the battle fleet. The giant Yorktown came over from the Atlantic Fleet. During the first months of war they made some minor strikes. They hit the Marshal Islands and Kwajalein Island. On May 7th, the battle of The Coral Sea took place and we lost the aircraft carrier Lexington. But the Japanese had been stopped. The Yorktown carrier had been severely damaged and it only took two days to fix her up. We had broken the Japanese code and found that they had designs on Midway Island. On the 4th of June 1942, down came the American "Hell" dive bombers. Admiral Yamagucci went down with his carrier and the Japanese fleet turned and headed home. We had won the course of WWII in the Pacific. I used our encoding/decoding equipment so our Admiral and officers knew what was going on as transmitted to and from them.

At the battle of Leyte Gulf, we only had one flat top left. The "Enterprise," our attack transport received orders to form up with an eight hundred ship fleet convoy and head for French Morocco, Africa. We were to land General Patton and the American forces at Casa Blanca and Safi. The German army had the French Foreign Legion trapped and had guns at their backs causing them to fight us (invaders) until they realized they were in bad circumstances.

On our way to Baltimore, the U.S.S. Leonard Wood interpreted wrongly a direction signal and it rammed our ship near the bow. I had copied code on the midnight watch so I was sound asleep when the collision occurred. I awoke with our ship listing forty-five degrees. The bow of the other ship was only a yard away. The water was pouring in and I had just got topside before they dogged down the hatches. As we left San Diego, a large taskforce of transport ships took off for Guadalcanal. Our ship headed into the harbor at Baltimore, MD and took ten days to be patched up, just in time to join the invasion of Morocco.

The Atlantic waters were full of German u-boats. The date of our landing, November 8, 1942, was near the date that my father left Oklahoma. General Patton and his forces went on towards Mara Ketch and we returned to Norfolk, Va. I had an eight day leave or vacation and I took a train to Oklahoma. I arrived there at midnight and left at four that same evening. My son, John R. jr. was 4 days old.

The Harris returned to San Diego and we took on about five hundred military nurses. We took them to Honolulu. In the spring of 1943, we loaded up with troops and headed for Attu in the Aleutian Islands. It was a scary invasion; there were nearly three thousand Japanese on Attu Island. On May 13th, we landed in the midst of a dense fog. You couldn't see for a foot in front of your face. It was very cold when our troops went in and their leather boots froze, which resulted in severe frostbite. Almost all of the Japanese were killed, but they had dug in hard. We lost nearly half of our troops and had to send in reinforcements. The reinforcement took over a week. After securing the island, our ship headed for Dutch Harbor, Kodiak and Ketchikan, Alaska. Then we went to Juneau. I remember that we received liberty (leave) and we bummed a ride on a fishing boat to town. The sailors got drunk and while returning to the ship one GOB hit another with a wet fish about two feet long. A big fight then broke out and half of the fish disappeared. Because of this situation, the second liberty party was canceled. We returned to Dutch Harbor, where a fishing boat captain discovered that I could repair his radio transmitter and receiver. I then proceeded to his boat and fixed the equipment. He proceeded to break open a new bottle of Johnny Walker whiskey. Later I was hauled drunk aboard the Harris in a cargo net.

We took on troops, but we had to wait because the Japanese fleet bore down on our fleet in the battle of the Aleutian Chain. My brother, Basil Huckaby, was aboard the heavy cruiser, The USS Salt Lake City. They fired broadside into the Japanese battleship, cruiser and taskforce. An eight inch shell hit the turret where Basil was located. He was slammed against the bulkhead and resulted in temporary insanity. As a result of this, he spent the next five years in a military hospital in Waco, Texas. He saved my life!

The Harris then returned to San Francisco and we took on a full complement of troops and returned to Kiska, the next island of the Rat Islands. Just as before, we crept into the shores of Kiska. We found that the Japanese had left the island the night before. Fires were still burning there. Our next assault was to take place on Kwajalein Island in the Marshall Islands. This was an atoll about twelve hundred miles south of Wake Island. Bunkers made from coconut logs and concrete protected the Japanese defenders. Their resistance to us was strong. At that point in time, I had been promoted to RM1c (radio man 1st class) and I was responsible for maintaining all the communication equipment for our landing party. We used the BC-610 and BC-612 transceivers. Sometimes they got wet with saltwater, so it was my duty to clean the transceivers and make sure that they were in operating condition. It took about a week, using reinforcements, to secure the island. The casualties were heavy and they kept coming back to the ship. The medical doctors used our mess hall as a "battlefield" operating room. They had to amputate arms and legs and also had to attend to those with severe burns. A great many lives were saved by sulfa drugs. My general quarter's station was outside the radio shack.

We returned to Honolulu and went into dry dock at Pearl Harbor. After scraping the barnacles off the bottom of the Harris, we radiomen then set out on our landing party. We took a case of beer up on the hill at YPO Point (a recreation park) and had a baseball game. It was our first recreation in two years. The Oahu freight passed the field just as the team was relieving themselves over the cliff to the tracks below. The Hawaiians sitting on the pineapples below got angry and shook their fists at the GOBs (slang for salior; who were laughing from above).

From the first sea duty, my job was to publish the ship's newspaper called "Press." Being a high speed code receiver and having good accuracy, I would put a stencil in the typewriter and tune in WCX, KOK, or World Press news stations. This way, all the sailors could know what was going on in the Atlantic European Theater and the Pacific (which wasn't censored). I would put Tokyo Rose on the ship's PA system so that the sailors could hear all of the propaganda. When the news was printing, many times the Captain would stand behind me and read it from over my shoulder. Whenever a burst of static came, I just kept on typing (for example, "Today, allied troops advanced over heavy terrain for....five kilometers under enemy fire to knock out enemy pill boxes, etc.) If I didn't complete it, the skipper would cough and moan. When the news was done, I took it down to the yeomen's and they printed it. Sometimes it would be three or four pages long. I was responsible for tuning in the short wave radio news, music, etc and for sending it over the PA system.

About two thousand five hundred troops were brought aboard and we set sail for the invasion of Eniwetok Island. This was one thousand miles northwest of Kwajalein Atoll. We were hedge hopping the Pacific Ocean, now twelve hundred miles southwest of Wake Island. It was another fight to the finish as the Japanese solidly entrenched behind fortifications of cocounut logs and hardening cement. As always, I made the combat grear war worthy and manned a fifty caliber AA gun outside the radio shack. It took about ten days and some reserve forces to rout the Japanese out of the island. All day and night the big battleships and helldivers shook the knolls. Finally, my eight radiomen (with transceivers) scrambled down the cargo nets to the LCVP landing boats. We had good communications and all worked excellently together. My group was responsible for sending information from shore to ship for the unloading; we would send messages for ammunition, blood plasma, food, cigarettes, etc. (until fully unloaded of trucks, half tracks, jeeps, etc.). We also did fire support data using a grid, it was possible to direct Navy guns and aircraft fire salvos. The wounded were dispatched to medical facilities aboard the transports.

Kwajalein was struck on December 4, 1943 and early in 1944 Mark Michner who was with Task Force fifty-eight, came into existence. There were six fleet carriers, six light carriers, eight fast battleships, six cruisers and thirty six destroyers. The U.S. Navy was now the most powerful navy in the world. The radar was in full use. My men had charge of the CIC (Combat Information Center). We had SC and SG radars. One had a PPI (Plan Position Indicator) and the other had distance measuring capability for important range measuring. We knew just how far away an object was. Once the Captain came running into the CIC and said, "Did you guys see that sailboat on the horizon?" and they replied, "Yes, Sir." He asked, "Did you go up and spot it with your eyes?"

We set sail for New Zealand and at Wellington New Zealand we picked up the Marines' provisions, combat gear, etc. We then headed for Tarawa (The Gilbert Islands). This was undoubtedly the most vicious battle ever in the history of the world. The Marines died by the hundreds. Some smart moves in landing saved entire regiments. They tricked the Japanese and hit it another place. There were dead bodies floating everywhere. My landing force lost half of their equipment. As I stood on the top deck, a six inch shell burst right over my head. I was hit and as a result of that incident, I still have some shrapnel in my head. We used all the reinforcements that we had. The Marines were dumped into beach water that was over their heads. Many of them drowned. They looked like turtles with their helmets floating just above the water. At that moment I thought, "Curtains, the farce has ended. I seek a Great Perhaps. All of this for another star in my Campaign Medals."

The dive bombers from off the carriers dumped ton after ton of bombs in the jungle. We had what seemed like thousands of casualties in our make shift hospital (the chow hall). It was like a living Hell on Earth. The imagination could not fathom this brutal devil like slaughter. When it was over, we trooped up and headed for Palau Island, Anguar and Ulithi. The Harris attacked these islands. It was bloody at Palau. On Ulithi, we found out that a bomb had killed the son of the native king of this island. He came aboard the ship with his wife and we gave him a lot of clothing and other things. On Anguar we met a lot of resistance, but the island was captured within a week. At that point, we were only fifteen hundred miles from Leyte in the Philippines. We took on more troops and headed in that direction by way of Sipan, Tinian and Guam in the Marianas. We hit Leyte with over two thousand five hundred troops. Our beach party landed with General MacArthur on his famous return.

The entire Japanese fleet bore down on the transports. We picked up a sailor who was floating in the water from one of the four jeep aircraft carriers that were sunk by the Japanese. The sailors name was Meyers and he was one of our radiomen who had transferred to the carrier. We rescued him with a boat hook and he was badly sunburned. We were really frightened and would have been more so if we had known that our old Pearl Harbor battleships had saved our lives. It was October 21st, the day MacArthur returned.

The Japanese sent out night fighters that were called "snoopers." That same day, the carrier planes hit Formosa. Several planes were lost. Our ground forces shot down forty planes that night using radar controlled guns. The Japanese put a torpedo into the English ship Canberra (one cold day during the Korean War, I, as a representative of the Americans, at the coronation of the current Queen Elizabeth II. The English were very pleased and gave me a big mug of brandy to drink).

On October 22nd, while we were still unloading at Leyte, the Japanese sent seven great battleships, nineteen cruisers, six carriers and thirty one destroyers from Brunei Bay (in Borneo) and some from Japan in order to attempt to "blow" us out of the water.

On October 24, 1944, this fleet was in our Philippine waters. They had hoped to get in among the merchant ships (us). It was like the scenario of a fox among the chickens in a shed and doing a great amount of damage.

As a defensive response, the first planes from the carriers Intrepid and Cabot damaged the cruiser Myoko. Yamato and Musashi shot down torpedo bombers and dive bombers. The Musashi trailed oil. The fourth wave of planes from the Essex, Lexington and the Enterprise hit with the strength of thirty planes, bombs and torpedoes. There were one hundred bombers from five American carriers and ten more torpedoes. The Japanese abandoned ship and half their crew was lost. The Musashi rolled over and sank with eleven hundred men on board. The Captain of the world's largest battleship was standing on the bridge. Admiral Halsey stopped pursuing the Kurita fleet and set out to attack Ozawa force.

Our attack transport, the Harris, and the other transports had landed General MacArthur. We had unloaded about half of our cargo when unbeknownst to us; we were looking down the barrel of an eighteen inch gun. The world's largest battleships, the Yamato and the Musashi were just a few miles away. Without a miracle, our lives would be finished and we'd be saying our last prayers. What could save us from the world's two largest battleships? We would have been blown out of the water. MacArthur's landing would have been a disaster and over fifty thousand American troops destroyed. The others had no chance for survival. What saved us?

Yamato's radar picked up the American planes and she had her one hundred and fifty aircraft guns ready. The planes from the Intrepid and the Cabot came in and the Yamato and Musashi battleships shot down some of the torpedo bombers and dive bombers. Two waves, one at 10:30 am and one at noon, were hit. The third wave (13:25) and the fourth (14:30) from the Essex and the Lexington came in. Admiral Ozawa tried to decoy the American forces away so that the Japanese could kill all of us and destroy all of the transports. We were right on the spot! On October 24th, at just about noon, Admiral Ozawa launched seventy planes against us. All but three of those planes were destroyed. That night the Japanese battleships slipped through the entire battleship force through the San Bernardino Strait and into the Philippine Sea. Their trick had worked and at that point we were goners. They would be able to destroy our transports (including the one that I was on). But something happened that saved us. At 08:15, planes from the American carriers appeared above the Ozawa battle force. A dozen planes from the American carriers had literally saved our lives. Only one American carrier, the Princeton, was sunk and their fleet was destroyed. Admiral Mitscher had sunk the sixty-three thousand ton battleship, the Yamato. We'd remember Task Force 58! The carrier Gambier Bay was sunk also. The Japanese, under Admiral Kurita, had struck the escort carrier group, thinking that it was a task force. It was then that Admiral Kurita fled through the San Bernardino Straits. We were saved by a little force of six escort carriers and eight destroyers, not the big ones.

Admiral Kurita decided against attacking our transports. One of them was the Harris, the one that I was aboard. Admiral Kurita wanted the fleet carriers. The carrier St. Louis was sunk. The Yamato had one thousand shells (eighteen inches) left. The Japanese Navy died in the fourth week of October 1944. Admiral Takijero invented the Kamikaze suicide attack. The escort carrier Independence, Belleau and St. Louis were sunk. Our ship and several others of the taskforce 135 steamed into Lynguyen Gulf at the Northern Luzon, Philippines. The suicide bombers were all over. Our mess hall was full of badly burned and wounded soldiers. After unloading in a landing at Lynguyen Gulf, we got underway and picked up a horned mine in our port Para Vane. The Captain has me radio the taskforce commander. I said, "Hello bluenose, this is Bench, have horned mine in port Para Vane, request disposition." He made his reply on the TBA (Talk Between Ships) transceiver and said, "Hello Bench. This is Bluenose. I'd get rid of it if it were me." A ship fitter, (a very brave sailor) climbed out of the yardarm and with a cable cutter, snipped the big steel cable. It floated free and when it drifted a little ways behind the (our) ship, the boatman mate Bull Russo shot it with a 30-06 rifle. It exploded and shot a geyser over one hundred feet high. It was huge, seven feet in diameter. Another six feet to the starboard, and we would have surely sunk. It contained several tons of very powerful explosives. As a result, four of us received the Presidential citation.

We took on a lot of casualties from the suicide kamikazes. For the tenth time that month I gave my blood in direct transfusions. Once, I remember, a transfusion to a red headed sailor who was badly burned in an attack He was pale and as my blood flowed into his veins: his cheeks began to take on a rosy color. Shortly after, they gave me a shot of whiskey. Russ Matthews, a Paramount Assistant Director, who was now an RM2c, gave blood with me that day and each time that they wanted O+ blood He really liked whiskey! Once when we were in dry dock, he got really drunk and jumped over the rail into the fifty-foot drop. But he grabbed the rail as he went over. It was then that we found out that he was also a stuntman for Paramount Pictures.

We took on some Marines and headed to Zambolies in the Mid Philippines to mop up on the remaining central Japanese forces in the Philippines. We sailed to the island of Okinawa. There was a lot of action and it was another "do or die" landing. The invasion of Okinawa remains clear in my memory. It happened on April 1, 1945, April Fool's Day! The troops went in at dawn. Heavy shelling from the carriers set the stage. Our landing boats went in only to meet heavy resistance on Red Beach. Just as soon as the troops landed, every available hand including myself began unloading ammunition. There were all kinds of different shells, mortar, grenade, howitzer (75mm and 105mms, hundreds of cases) and the guns themselves. While the troops were securing beaches at Naha, we were giving everything we had to rid our transport ship (Harris) of these supplies. The cargo nets were swinging constantly as we filled them with shells, rockets and small arm ammunition. I labored continuously for eighteen hours that day. At about ten that night, a Japanese shell hit the mountainous pile of explosives. For twenty miles around, there was a continuous bombardment. It was the greatest pyrotechnic explosion that anyone had ever seen. All night long, thousands upon thousands of explosives boomed and lit up the sky for miles around. The earth shook and trembled like an earthquake.

The following day we worked with an intense effort because of the fear that the kamikaze suicide planes would appear. Our fate would be sealed if one Japanese plane were to land in the number two or three hatch where half of the ammo was packed full to the bottom deck. Fortunately, God was with us and we got the stuff off and unloaded it at Naha on red and blue beaches. We piled up in isolated batches for fear of another enemy hit. Trip after trip and load after load, we worked furiously at unloading our attack transport. On the third day a lone Japanese plane showed up on the horizon. One of the corsairs swooped down and shot it. The plane crashed into the seas. On the fifth day another zero or their later model flew high in the clouds. It was jumping around and over five hundred ships began shooting at it with every gun available-battleships, tin cans (destroyers), transports and even tugboats with fifty caliber machine guns. The sky was full of thousands of tracers, but we had some shells with proximity explosives in them. The cruisers had fire control radar and when those cruisers would fire, the shell would burst seeming only inches away. In spite of the hundreds of thousands of bullets and shells, we didn't hit the kamikaze! On May 14th, one dived out of a cloud above the carrier Enterprise. The pilot turned the plane over on its back and dived down the elevator shaft. His bomb exploded five decks below the bridge and blew the elevator forward about four hundred feet in the air. The damage was so great that she couldn't operate her planes and it was feared that she would sink. It took seventeen minutes to put out first the fires and a half an hour to put out. Admiral Mitchner transferred his flag to the Randolph and the Enterprise went home. The kamikazes kept it up. The Japanese knew the carriers were the most formidable weapons in our fleet.

Mitchner was bombed off the Bunker Hill with a loss of three hundred forty six men and thirteen of his own staff. On February 2, 1947, in the Norfolk Virginia Navy Hospital, he slipped his anchor chain (died). On June 16, 1944, Admiral Bull Halsey took over the third fleet. In a month's time, he knocked out four thousand five hundred enemy aircraft and sank four hundred fifty ships; an unbelievable record! He struck at Tokyo in June 1945.

After Okinawa we went to sea and rode out the most powerful hurricane. There were many ships washed up on the beaches! Then it was off to Iwo Jima. The Harris was not in the first phase of the attack. At that time, I was promoted to Chief Petty Officer and replaced Chief Good.

It was at Iwo Jima about the middle of August 1945, that the atomic bomb was dropped on Hiroshima and Nagasaki, Japan on Kyushu Island. It was on August 20th that Japan surrendered and VWII was over. President Roosevelt had died in the spring and Harry Truman was now President of the United States of America.

My Navy enlistment only had ten months left. Based on honorable service my orders read as follows: "Proceed to Navy Electronics Training Center at Dearborn, Michigan at the Ford Motor Plant at Willow Run in Dearborn." Upon finishing school in January 1946, I was sent aboard a LSD (Landing Ship Dock) It was LSD-8 a ship which carried about ten LCVP's in the stern, which could be flooded and the tailgate opened and the landing craft cruise to the beachhead in an assault operation. This ship (the LSD8, the Ashland) sailed for San Diego, California. Not to say the least was very happy. The first Sunday, I stood captain inspection. The Captain, when he saw my medals/ribbons, gave me a quick interview and said, "You belong in top operations." That afternoon an Admiral Barge came with orders to transfer me to the USS Wasatch. I was to be in charge of the entire communications flag of Comtrans div 19. I had to provide battle plans for 208 Communications personnel. The ship was a combat center for command and control by the Division Admiral. It was hard work because you had to supervise a large group of men and their duties. You'd have to report on a daily basis to the "Old Man" of the 19th division. If anything was delinquent or lacking, he wanted to know about it! It was then that I'd made up my mind to request a discharge.

The largest reason being- every week they gave me shore patrol duty on the streets of San Diego, California. Walking an eight hour shift is really tiresome; your feet feel like they would collapse also I had blisters on my toes. Here was the worst dirty part of the assignment; the round (beat) called for me to help throw the drunken sailors into the padded SP wagon who had been thrown out of the bars onto the streets. What a nasty job that was and sometimes I had to at the close of my watch help throw them under the showers with their clothes on at the SP headquarters. All this repulsive work was to keep the local police from throwing the sailors into their vehicles and throwing them in their jails making more trouble for the Navy.

My discharge came on June 14, 1946 at the Terminal Island, CA. The recruiting officer told me to join the reserves and get a paycheck monthly so I signed up. About five minutes later an announcement came over the audio system "All newly enlisted reservists lay down to the sickbay and get your shots." Disgustedly I followed those orders!

John's Family Son Jr. Year
Long Beach Ca.
1943

Book Three

CHAPTER 4

END OF WWII AND START OF KOREA WAR
JOHN'S ACTIVE MILITARY SERVICE (WEDNESDAY NIGHTS) BETWEEN JUNE 1946 AND JUNE 1950

From then on each time that I received my paycheck in the reserves there was a pharmacist mate standing on each side of the pay line to inoculate me for something or maybe just for practice?

For the next four years on every Wednesday evening from seven to ten p.m. my job in the active reserves was to train other reserve Navy radiomen to become skilled radio operators and repair the equipment. I lived then in Long beach, California and traveled about twenty miles to the Los Alamitos Navy Air Station for duty. Several of my students went on to become ham (amateur) radio operators. Little did we dream there would ever be another war because WWII and the Atomic bomb had ended war forever? My service in the reserve (active) included four summer trips, each for two weeks. One to Acapulco, Mexico, another to Honolulu on a transport ship where we lost a sailor falling overboard during "horseplay." The ship stopped and searched for him, but we never found him…Another trip was on the USS Destroyer Bush DD-685.

This concluded my active reserve Navy time between the end of WWII and start of the Korean conflict which I found out "another war" now called the "forgotten war"

MY DAYTIME JOBS BETWEEN JUNE 1946 AND JUNE 1950 (END OF WWII TO START OF THE KOREAN WAR)

During the four years following WWII when I was in the naval reserves, I found employment as a petroleum engineer with the E.B. Hall oil company, a contractor for the Union Pacific Railroad. We were drilling oil wells and shipping the oil to buyers on Terminal Island at San Pedro, CA. The land was bought by a representative in a bar and when they surveyed the land, found it submerged in sea water. Needless to say, he lost his job. However in 1937 a sea wall was built and it became dry land. Tests were made and found that oil existed. The first oil well was a gusher! It produced over 37,000 barrels on day one. As the story goes, the representative was offered his job back but he refused it. From that day on over 700 wells were drilled by E.B. Hall contractor, who also stored, measured and shipped it.

My experience with my father in the oil business made me a good employee. My knowledge and use of advanced mathematics was very advantages to me. Every 75' the drill bit was removed and a camera was lowered down the hole where as a special camera took a picture and I used trigonometric reading to plot where the bit was. This was vital information because it was very important "not to be taking oil from under your neighbors land." A guy nicknamed whipstock Bill invented a device called a whipstock to direct and steal oil. I plotted individual well output on log/log desi trig graph paper.

When returning from Korea according to the VA, I was supposed to get my job back. After two and a half years fighting in Korea with an honorable discharge, I came home to find my job gone! General Petroleum Company had bought the company and the office building was torn down! This was a mental blow to me and I recalled the four years I had worked there. From the time I started and worked on the PBX (telephone exchange), type engineering reports, using the marchant calculator and then doing tests on the oil like specific gravity, bottom settlements (BS), and measurements by the centrifugal device All in all it was so sad.

MY PART TIME JOB BETWEEN JUNE 1946 AND JUNE 1950 (END OF WWII AND START OF KOREAN WAR)

During the four year period working as petroleum engineer, on each Saturday I had a part time job with the Salvation Army at Long Beach, Ca repairing donated radio and electrical items in exchange of a percentage of their sale price. They had sponsored the release of a prisoner to help me fix the damaged items. He seemed such an honest guy and told me he had been a short order cook. One day I passed by a vacant restaurant with a for rent sign on it and rented it, bought a cash register and put him cooking my bought food. A month later when checking for my money, I found him and the cash register gone! I really thought the guy was sincere and honest, mistaken credulity…

MY FOUR YEAR STUDY AND COMPLETION OF COURSE AT THE LONG BEACH ACADEMY OF ART (MONDAY AND FRIDAY NIGHTS) FROM JUNE 1946 TO JUNE 1950 (END OF WWII TO START OF KOREA)

After four years of fighting in WWII where 475,000 military men died (Americans) of which at least 100,000 died during campaigns in the pacific area that I was in, my thoughts turned to God very strongly. He must have a reason to keep me alive and for some good purpose?

God had given me a talent and a gift, so why not use it to do something for mankind. Not just doodling but highly creative art and beauty like the hands of God had done with wonder and breath taking splendor.

How fortunate it was, I enrolled in the Long Beach Academy of Art located at Long Beach, Californina. Classes were held on Monday and Friday each week. It was as if God alone had lead me to this great school of art, the classes were under the supervision of Mr. Carl Sethaller of Austrian decent extreamly brilliant. He taught us about the Old masters, modernists, impressionists, surrealist and the dadoist, He hired the most beautiful models for us to draw, we were so busy drawing and painting them our minds were on our work instead of ogling (eyeing them with amorously or provactaively glances). The most enlightening thing we learned from his teaching was how God's designs followed a specific mathematical system called Dynamic Symmetry, sometimes referred to as the Golden Ratio The greek artists discovered it and use it to design statues like Venice De Milo, buildings like the Parthenon and many vases. All having the magic size of God's design. Those ancient greeks were great thinkers and understood there was an intelligent designer. Our teacher had a big sea shell and using the lines and measuring such we could multiply and divide, it was a slide rule. Just like the logarithmic slide rule I used in my engineering calculations. God is dynamic. God is not static. We learned the design found in nature. The flowers e.g.: a sunflower seeds fall in a circle 21 lines in one direction and 13 lines in opposite direction. Dividing 21 by 13 we have 1.618. We could use a canvas 10" x 16.18" or reciprocal approximately 8" x 10". What is all this dynamic symmetry about for me? Knowing how God designed nature, our skeleton proportions help us draw better figures and plant or flowers. For the first time I realized if my paintings and art followed criteria set forth by our creator they would have eye appeal. As a result, my paintings have won many blue "first place" and a couple of "best of the show awards." There is no way I could have had the success without giving God, His Son Jesus and the Holy Spirit "full credit" for their invention in my life and art.

Upon completing my art classes, only two weeks later on the 20th of June 1950 the Korean conflict started and I received a telegram stating "Report to eleventh Naval District, San Diego, California within the next 24 hours" to catch a ship headed for Korea.

Book Four

CHAPTER 5

We sailed to Korea aboard the USS LSMR 403 a rocket launch and fire that had seventy-five pound super penetrating explosive rockets. The ship had thirteen rocket mounts and could fire them four times per second for a total of fifty-two rockets per second. The ship would visibly rise up in the water when they were fired. That attack ship was equipped with large electronic equipment. One thing that I found to be interesting was that there were teletype machines that copied the SKED messages so that we didn't need an operator to type the code in as was done in WWII. I was chief radioman petty officer in charge.

The ship's crew included eight radiomen and two in the flag compliment. The ship went to Sasebo in Japan where we took on a shipload of rockets. Upon fueling, we sailed to Korea, about the 39th parallel near Sonjin. It was here that we fired every rocket that we had on the ship. The rocket firing ship then proceeded to Sasabo and Kyushu, Japan and then reloaded with rockets. The Japanese worked all day and half of the night to refill the magazines. It took about two weeks to replenish the USS LSMR 403 and in the meantime, the ship's crew had an extended liberty. Most of the personnel ended up at the local dance hall named the "Hakubatan." The ship went on picket duty. Most of the winter, we sailed around a small island called "Wonampondo." The navy commander didn't want the North Koreans to occupy the island. Our ship was given the task of relieving the South Koreans from technically keeping the island under surveillance. All winter long, we shuttled back and forth between Sasabo and the North Korean mainland to bomb about the 38th parallel and to guard "Wonampondo" Island. The temperature, at that time, was well below zero and the men on duty topside wore their pea coats and rubberized foul weather jackets. The Quartermaster on duty would, every so often, come into the radio shack to warm up and listen to me play my ukulele.

The Red Chinese entered the war and it soon escalated into a full size battlefield. Our ground troops had suffered big losses. It became a skirmish from hill to hill. General MacArthur got in an argument with President Truman and was released form his command. He bowed out saying, "old soldiers never die, and they just fade away."

The LSMR 403 was called upon to bombard the area above the 38th parallel about Sonjin (North Korean mainland). We went back to Sasabo and filled the ammo lockers to their tops with seventy-five pound rockets. The Japanese laborers worked night and day carrying the rockets on their shoulders down into the magazine. The ship got underway with its sister ship, the LSMR 404 to Sonjin for the purpose of taking some of the pressure off of the allied troops fighting just below. I remember how spooky it was the night that we went into the harbor above Sonjin. At about 21:00 (9:00pm), the two rocket ships were in position to bombard the area under attack. We were in a closed harbor and could only navigate by radar. When the command to "start firing" was issued, the five inch forward gun fired, the concussion knocking out the radar. The hatch on the main deck had inadvertently been left open. The concussion shattered the modulator tube in radar. Now we were "sitting ducks" for the North Korean shore guns. It was so black that night. I remember getting another tube from the spare parts locker and the Electronic Technician (second class) installed it. When power was regained, the radar worked perfectly. We fired all of the rockets aboard ship and then "ran for it" along with our sister ship (LSMR 404). Next day reconnaissance planes report a couple bordellos destroyed.

I had now received the Korean Service Medal, one star and the United Nations Service Medal. A short time afterwards, the war ended in a truce. After one year, five months and eighteen days, of active sea duty in Korea, the ship returned to the United States. We had been in the initial landing of troops in support of the Inchon and Pusan landings. For me, the most frightening part of the Korean War was the "radar" episode. The worst part was the cold. True it was the "Coldest War" and the forgotten war. Our ship, the USS LSMR 403 was at Inchon landing.

My enlistment in the Active reserve was complete on August 22, 1952. At that point I had put in twelve years, two months and twelve days of faithful service to my country. That had included four summer reserve trips. I had earned another star on my Presidential Citation Ribbon.

Book Five

CHAPTER 6

MERCHANT MARINES WORLD TRAVLES

The job that I was supposed to get when I got home and the office that I was supposed to report to were not to be found. The company was gone and there was no more oil. I started looking for a job and found one with Douglas Aircraft Company. It was in the R&D area of the Engineering section. We did the research on the RB66 air Force jet fighter bomber and tests for jet engines for the DC6 and DC7.

In the evenings I went to the Crawford School of Marine Engineering and obtained my U.S. Coast Guard Officer license along with my U.S. Telephone and Telegraph Commercial license (plus my General Amateur license). Now I had the qualifications to be a Commercial Shipboard Licensed Operator. One afternoon I received a phone call from the Port Captain asking me if I'd take a ship called the SS Anthony to Walvis Bay, South Africa. Douglas gave me an extended leave of absence and after packing my sea bag, I sailed at midnight from San Pedro Harbor. The next morning I found out it was a Greek tramp steamer and only one sailor understood the English language. I was informed that the Greek radio operator had deserted the ship. There was no difficulty in operating the communication and electronic equipment, as it was a USA Liberty ship sold and sailing under the Panamanian flag. I spent most of my time learning the Greek language. I sent and received routine messages daily. Our captain, Dimetres Beis, was very interested in the weather, fixes on the direction finder, SOS signals when the automatic distress gear rang a big bell in his room, on the bridge and in my quarters.

I operated the depth finder (sonar) as well as the LF and HF radio equipment. The Greeks called me Marconi! Each day at noon, I'd send a message to the Greek owners in London, England. I would give our position report and I'd copy the WX reports and keep in touch with the other steamships, etc. After refueling in Trinidad, the ship sailed towards Walvis Bay in South Africa. After a week at sea, the first SOS came through. An English ship loaded with cotton was on fire. It seemed impossible to put out the fire in the bales of cotton. Would it burn underwater? Yes! We set an intercept course a few degrees off ours. Another ship close by and nearer, led the English ship to Walvis Bay.

We unloaded half of the lumber that we had taken on in Vancouver, Canada along with several tons of salted herring fish. The natives were very dark and they all looked alike to me. Later, I could see, as with white people, they had different features. Upon leaving, we waved goodbye to IIza, who had given us a short wave radio. They let me install it in the officer's mess quarters. So that I could interpret the news, one Greek sailor made me a Greek/English dictionary. I'd already had a good understanding of the Japanese language. One time in Mormagaro India one sailor got an immunization shot in his buttock with a rusty or dirty needle. I had to treat him with Potassium Permanganate, purple oxidizer and disinfectant swabs. The flesh eventually rotted leaving a gaping hole. In time, new flesh grew back to close up the gap. Because all the drugs were labeled in English, the pharmacy was under my control. I received extra pay as the acting pharmacist. Once I sent out an SOS for help when we were in the Red Sea. Tel Aviv answered me and had to treat a sailor intravenously with a corimine and glucose solution and it worked. I remember when a sailor got his foot smashed by a beam, I set it and taped it up. Two weeks later when we arrived in Chiba Harbor, Tokyo, I took him to the Japanese doctor and I translated from Greek into Japanese and vice versa. The Japanese doctor shook his head in disbelief. They took x-rays and found that it was just right. He asked me how I knew how to set it and I told him that I had studied anatomy for four years in an art school and I molded it as the opposite foot with the big toe on the inside. He replied, "Subarashi" (splendid) and took a big gulp of his alcoholic disinfectant to calm his amazement.

Once Anastasus, the chief cook officer got a case of dysentery and I went over to Alexandria Egypt and got some penicillin. This cured him from some other disease that he had gotten from some raw oysters. I also cured Polecrasas with sulfa powder (sulfanilamide). There were all kinds of medicines left over from when the ship was in Merchant service ten years earlier in 1944. I spent much time study of the medical books left behind, along with my book of Shakespearian writings (complete).

I remember well the storm that struck us in the English Channel and I'd received twenty-four SOS calls in one afternoon as ships were running aground. All we could do that day was pray. Our captain stood on the bow for hours transfixed, staring into the dense fog. The ship went on to Port Elizabeth and unloaded more lumber. Then we went up the East coast of Africa to Lorinzo marks and Beria, South Africa and unloaded the rest of the lumber. We headed back to Port Elizabeth and loaded on a shipload of grain. We began a forty day voyage to Hamburg, Germany, unloaded the grain and took cargo to Hull, England. From there we sailed on to the following places: Glasgow, Scotland, Marseilles, France, (I visited Robert Burns home and Jolly Begger Bar, and Paris France), through the Suez Canal to Karachi, Pakistan, GOA Mormago, Portugal (now India), Chiba Harbor in Japan - then back to Vancouver, Canada, again to Marseilles, France, Saigon Indo China. We delivered tanks, barbed wire, ammo and war cargo to Saigon for the French Foreign Legion. We sailed up fifty miles of river with our Greek sailors, South Vietnamese military and manning fifty caliber machine gun outside the radio shack. Once the North Vietnamese did fire on us, but luckily there were no casualties. I saw numerous Vietnamese working in the watery rice fields and I wondered if they knew a Communist from Democrat. I was sure that in fifty years they (if alive) would be standing there in the water up to their butts in that same rice paddy. I wondered what Democracy would do for them.

We went back to GOA, where Indians clad with only rag around their behinds shoveled iron ore onto the barges; then took it to the ship and shoveled it into the cargo nets. The Greeks winched it in and dumped it into the holes. The ore was very heavy and we were in danger of sinking. But we traveled on past Singapore to Tokyo and on the way, near Formosa, American fighter planes buzzed over us to make certain that we weren't Communist Chinese invasion forces. When they saw the Panamanian flag, they left. This happened in 1954 and it was in 1955 at the Bay of Tompkin that the war between Vietnam and the United States began. I was in Saigon when the De-In-Ben-Fou, French Indo China pullout took place. We sailed on to the United States and hit a bad storm in the North pacific. The empty ship weathered some forty foot waves. The captain said to "keep SOS on standby" and we sailed on to Vancouver, Canada where we loaded up with lumber and sailed for Emden, Germany. There we unloaded and left for Norfolk, Virginia in the United States. In Norfolk, we loaded up with coal that we were to take back to Emden. While in Norfolk, I took a tech rep job with Philco and they let me take the "Anthony" back to Emden, Germany and train another radioman (an Irishman) that would take my place upon returning to the port of Norfolk, Va., for yet another incredible life story.

Book Six

Philco, July 5, 1955-1967

It was a sad moment when leaving that old Greek tramp steamer. All the crew members gathered at the gang plank on the SS Anthony, they shook my hand and yelled "Herete" (Goodbye).

Leaving the ship I took a bus to Philadelphia, Pa on July 5, 1955 and reported to the Philco Technical Representative headquarters at 22nd and Legigh Avenue. Philco trained me for three months on how to install, operate and trouble shoot their new 24 channel microwave telephone and telegraph microwave system, in France for the United States Air Force. The system joined with the Army's at Fountainbleau, France and went to England. It also connected with American air force bases at Dreux and Evereux France.

There was a lot of work and travel associated with keeping the system operative. I was responsible for the alignment of the microwave dishes, emergency power diesel generators, wiring and tuning the klystrons, plus all the associated major and minor items.

The cold war with Russia was now in full force and the fear of an atomic war was at its peak. The atomic fallout dust from nuclear tests in the south Pacific had caused the grass and plants to wither.

The microwave system cost over ninety million dollars, but it was amazing it was terminated on an army hand cranked telephone, a drab green canvas trench warfare telephone hanging from the main frame but it worked. The main trouble was the French Electric Power which at that time was not 100% reliable. Once when checking on the English Terminal at their command post, I was very surprised to see them sitting around watching the Follies Bigere on their tv they had it piped over the microwave system. They seemed to be more concerned with condition flesh color than red.

I wore out one English and two French automobiles while running up and down the telephone system for over two and a half years while keeping it operational. Later Prime Minister Degauile ousted American forces from France. The American bases were shut and torn down and the equipment went to salvage. I met a sergeant who said, "I had to bulldoze a lot of the stuff in the ground." Upon returning from France in 1957 to PHILCO Headquarters they assigned me a very interesting job teaching advanced electronics at Fort Monmouth, NJ. at the Army training school. The course started with the basics and ended up training them to operate huge radio transmitters some 50 Kilowatt. In addition they learned to repair and operate the new single sideband Western Electric set. Some of the transmitters were so large they were tuned by servo systems.

There were some scary moments we had in that class. Once a student while tuning the huge transmitter failed to reduce the power and a blinding arc flashed through the observation window. It was the first time I ever saw a man run while standing still. Another time a student was tuning the powerful transmitter I dove to the off switch. Looking thru the outside window there was a soldier dipping his hand in the dummy load barrel we used to terminate the fifty thousand watts while tuning. When the transmitter was keyed his hand went up and down in sync. Luckily he was not electrocuted. I put in a work order to build a fence around the dummy load.

A year later I returned to headquarters as the teaching position I held went to the lowest bidder and Philco lost the contract. In those days there was a lot of competition in the field of engineering as most all companies were engaged in providing technical representatives. Philco had a new job for me and four other tech reps. We were going to Saudi Arabia and work for ARAMCO the American Arabian Oil company.

Our visas were completed and we took the ARAMCO plane to Beruth, Lebanon. Our task was to install a telemetry system along a twelve hundred mile length of a pipe line from Kuwait oil fields along a 30 inch diameter pipe to loading terminals at Tyre and Sidon on the west coast, in addition there had to be a VHF radio channel one hundred foot towers with twenty three element yagi antennas so automobiles could have communication facilities.

The purpose of this communication and control system was to also control the pumping stations located about a hundred miles apart. A station would stop and the others keep pumping the pipe would burst and there would be oil on a great length of desert sands. By controlling the pumping stations at Turaif, Kusuma, Badana, Jalamed and Ulagula there was a huge financial gain. Instead of getting 200,000 barrels a day through a pipe, with control, now up to 500,000 barrels was possible. There were both Arab and Jewish workers. The Arabs would climb down the tower and say their prayers in the sand. They really enjoyed my American cigarettes.

Back in the late fall of 1957 the Russian Sputnick was set in orbit. I saw it once. When leaving Beruth on the ARAMCO plane speeding down the runway, shells were exploding behind us. That was in the year 1957, 54 years ago and things are still unsettled. I was in the middle of the 4th war of my life. Did 6 mo. programming PHILCO TRANSAC 2000 Computer for air defence of America. (It had 56,000 transistors)

May 15, 1959 Philco obtained a contract with the US Air Force for my services, with the Ground electronic Engineering Installation Agency () located at Griffith Air Force base in Rome, NY. After an interview I was assigned to the Standards Branch.

My 12 ½ years of US Navy Service had taught me a lot about standards, when going from ship to ship the same radios, transmitters, test equipment and other items were the same, the instruction books, radar, sonar, direction finders were standardized. This was a big asset for the Navy and the training was simplified. When a new item was introduced in the inventory it went on procurement bid and contract awarded. This stopped buying every different piece of equipment and having a huge number of spare parts. The Navy even had a bureau for standardizing their systems, facilities, equipment and the entire communication and electronic structure. The American Bureau of standards has been a great help for the American people. Today in America we have two sets of standards for many tools and minor items, called the metric system. This doubles the cost of outfitting the repairmen, except some American and metric tools are near enough to be interchangeable.

My task was to assist, along with other engineers in our section to compile and publish after review, the standard facilities, their equipment components (major items), minor items and hardware, along with drawings and technical orders. The end result was a standard facility equipment list (SFEL) and it was published. In addition, my responsibility was to publish the "Facility Planning Guide" which took the SFELS associated with a typical installation and publishing this facility for the planner and programmer and engineer. In addition we developed a list of materials catalogue (LOM) it included every minor items and hardware and had a LOM number, and the manufacturers that made the item, thus allowing procurement, when replacing it to avoid sole-source buy. The project engineer would make a site survey to determine if any changes were necessary. Then prepare a SCHEME (installation package) for review by the review section and installation team, and send it to CESAC (communications electronics supply and control) for their review and shipment.

Retired Colonel Michael Forte was our standards division commander and gave us standards engineers commendation and appreciation awards, later after having successfully organizing and managing our standards division he advanced to a top management position with a major electronics corporation.

PHILCO TECH-REP 1964-1967

Everything went fine with our standards except about two years later after having saved considerable money for the defense budget, we were in trouble. The defense planners introduced monstrous radars, some of them six stories high with large antennas and the over the horizon ones with antennas nearly as big as a football field. The only way out was called "Turn Key" where we had to resort to the builder to provide training, spare parts and service and personnel to keep it operating. However, it was decided that our installation personnel had the "In House" capability to do certain repairs. For example, the Air Force technicians could replace the six inch bearings in the radar antenna turntable, thus saving considerable money. I assume that our or some equivalent is still in operation. If so give thanks for those standard's engineers back in the 1960's for being so "future minded."

CIVIL SERVICE 1967-1986

GEEIA moved to Tinker AFB in 1970 and the National Communication Agency (NCA) assumed command at Griffith in Rome, NY. Later the 485th engineering took over. I had worked as a Tech Rep for PHILCO/PHILCO-Ford until 1967 when I took a position with the Civil Service and retired on January 2, 1986.

My Civil service employment was very interesting as it took me to many places in the United States, England and Germany. It also took me to Turkey. My health went bad and I started jogging in the spring of 1974 during my lunch hour and in the evenings at home. My wife Betty retired from Rome Cable in 1980 after 21 years as a secretary and became the manager of our retirement manufactured housing park.

Book Seven

CHAPTER 7

SUMMARY OF ULTRAMARATHONS

It was in the spring of the year 1974 when I had returned from Colarado springs, Colorado, having finished engineering a major project and supervising the installation of computers for the air defence of America, when I developed angina pains. I went to the emergency room and they told me "go make out a will before you go to see your family doctor!" Instead I went to see an electrocardiograph operator who confirmed the diagnosis. My family doctor told me that I was over weight and my blood pressure was like a "hydraulic ram." Frightened, I returned to work and luckily received some very helpful advice and consolation from a fellow engineer who was a par golfer and marathon runner. Naturally he advised me to start an exercise program and stick with it. I walked faithfully for about a month when I was caught in a rain storm and ran for about less than a hundred yards to shelter. I remember "my breath was hot as a blow torch." However, I prayed about it and got the message to "keep on trying for it." I kept up my walking routine for another month and then jogged and walked for a couple more months. I lost several pounds and my 225 pounds went down to 200. My blood pressure decreased almost to normal.

I adopted my fellow engineer, Tom Hovey as my health adviser and coach, who continued to train and help me. He also gave me encouragement. At this period in my rehab, I joined the Roman Runners, a group who would meet once a week and run, jog or walk for 5 kilometers (3.1 miles).

My first race was from the gym on Griffith AFB to their picnic area 5K (3.1 miles). My daughter then age 21 hobbled along with me and sprinted in the last fifty feet to make me finish in last place and got the "turtle award."

At the Roman Runners club then managed by radio executive Mr. Carl Eilenberg we had fun runs weekly and my endurance and speed increased to such a large degree that also by working out at the YMCA evenings. In addition, I'd run about 6 miles during my one hour lunch break and still have time to gobble up half dozen bananas for the strength of a gorilla. Additionally, went on a diet of oatmeal for breakfast which amusingly gave me the speed of a racehorse.

It was at the time Carl who had become mayor of Rome gave me a nick name "The Incredible Huck." In less than two years I had climbed up the running ladder to become a fitness animal. Five years later I was a legend. I started doing the crazy running's things eg: when running the Skylon marathon from Buffalo to Niagra Falls, Cananda I fell over a orange road marker resulting in a stress fracture in the left foot, I completed the marathon, drove the car over night, sometimes hanging my left foot out the car window in the cold night air to keep the swelling down. Then at Staten Island NYC I stuck it in a toilet, flushed about 20 times and ran the NYC marathon, 26.2 miles in about 3 1/2 hours. The date was November 21/22, 1978. In 1977 I had run over 2,600 miles and completed four marathons including Rome, Boston, Skylon and Jersey shore (Asbury Park).

In 1978 I passed the 3,107 mi (5000 km) milestone. Like New York city to San Francisco and completed 12 marathons. Plus my first ultra-marathon the grueling JFK Ultra-Marathon over the Appalachian mountains for a distance of 50.2 miles, from Boonville to Harpers Ferry, then along the Patomac and C&O canal to Dam 44 and back to Boonville in nine hours. I remember passing old fox holes, one perhaps my grandfather used when he fought in the Civil War. A more detailed description is found on the chapter in this book in chapters describing in detail my Ultra-marathons (long distance races over 26.2 miles). I ran the JFK on 11/18/78 and again in 11/17/79.

January 17, 1979 I completed the Major's jewelers 62.2 miles (100 km) ultra marathon in Miami, Florida in 12 hours 10 minutes and 45 seconds.

May 22 1979 I ran the first notable marathon. Where Pheidippides in the war between Greece and Persia, ran some 25 tortuous miles carrying the news of the Athenian army's miraculous defeat of the 300,000 Persian warriors on the plain of Marathon Greece in 90 BC, arriving in Athens he announced "Rejoyce We Conquer!" Thereon he collapsed and died on the spot.

The Athens newspaper read "The most colorful runner in the group was near 60 year old John Huckaby billed as the "Incredible Huck." "A computer engineer from New York State. He was rejected in a heart screening test about six years ago and was given a life expectancy of less than six months. He took up walking, then running to regenerate his body."

With 16 marathons and two ultra marathons to his credit, the undefeatable lovable Huck assertively announced that I intended to run the Pheidippides course three times. Yes, three back to back times in the same day (78.6 miles). There was some speculation about whether I had popped one too many vitamins. The finishing point was the all marble Athens Stadium capable of seating 30 thousand spectators.

The first runner to finish the marathon was Michael Duncan, 29 from San Mateo, California. His time was 2.33.36.

When the trophies were presented later that evening at a joyous poolside party on the roof of the Athens hotel, there was one notable omission; Myself. I was still running and true to my word. By midnight I had covered the course three times (78.6 miles) incredible.

In that era there were perhaps over 20,000,000 runners and jogging addicts in America in the late 1970's. Running had become habit forming and if I did not go out for his daily run, I would get down in the dumps. I craved the oxygen high, where I would sprint up a hill and then relax on the level ground this was like a shot in the arm. Steroids were not invented way back in those days so I just had to do my thing legally and the only thing was to just gut it out. I did find something to help my in my long distant running. It was called carbohydrate loading where I would eat only proteins for five days before the race and the night before the race to eat a big bowl of spaghetti which produced a high level of blood sugar and my muscles would just "slurp" this glycogen up and store it in my muscles. If you run near utter exhaustion it could give you an edge in the race. I also took a lot of vitamins. There were several other electrolyte replacement glucose drinks used by athletes at that time such as ERG, Gooken Aid and Gatoraid. They didn't taste very good though. Actually they were composed of the same substances as liquid sweat. Replacing if taken in time the body fluids lost due to perspiring.

In July 1979 I completed the western states endurance (the ultimate challenge) 100 mile run in less than 30 hours. I ran over the high Sierra Nevada Mountains from Squaw Valley to Auburn, California to finish the race. "I ran up and down hills for over 20,000 feet during the race, I remember, "this is like running up and down the empire state building 20 times over the 100 miles snake and bear infested trails." The 1960 Winter Olympics were held there.

January 12, 1980 I completed the Hawaiian triathlon a grueling 2.4 mile rough water course, 112 mile bike ride and a 26.2 mile marathon. The Hawaii news week wrote "senior ironman John Huckaby runs for life." I had run in competitions from Florida to Lake Placid and from Boston to California. My life style may not be the answer to everyone's problems, but it sure has proved that a human being can become just as fit and go just as far as his ambitions and dreams. People have said, John Huckaby is truly "Incredible." Prime ingredients in my lifestyle are running, healthy eating and putting faith in the Almighty. With enough determination I can do anything!" It took me over 12 hours to finish the Ironman Ultra Hawaiian marathon. I had been washed ashore by big waves twice during the swim, crashed three times on my bicycle—wrecking donated bikes- and finally finishing the marathon run with so much skin missing from my sparce frame that "I looked like a hamburger."

April 20-21 1980 the race officials had changed the qualifying times of the Boston marathon for senior citizens over age 60 years for both men and women by 20 minutes. Going from 3 hours thirty minutes to 3 hours ten minutes. This was priming them for a heart attack. I protested by running the Boston course four times non stop (104.8 miles). Only one senior citizen officially finished the 1980 Boston marathon. He was from Vensueila, South America. Thanks to myself, the standards were changed. It was a bad finish for the women because a woman who only ran a couple of blocks jumped into the race and won it unfairly. Her name was Rosie Rusiz! It caused a lot of disorder and she stole all my thunder.

October 31 to November 2, 1980, starting Halloween night, in Memphis, Tennessee, I threw a sheet over my head, not having a costume, and ran in several races called the "Goblin Gallop."

The first event was a 2 ½ mile costume race. It was won by a large dog in a Full Moon runner's T shirt. It took me nearly 25 minutes to finish. I won a t shirt for winning the unknown comic category.

The twelve hour "fun run" started at 1:00 am and ended at 1:00 pm. I got 8th place and had run timed for exactly 51 miles and could have done more except saving some energy for the next six km run a speed race. I had just finished running 53.5 miles when toeing the line of the 10km race. It took me 51 minutes to run that 10km speed run. I picked out my third t shirt and went to the Memphis state university field track to start the 24 hour ultra marathon, which started at 4:30 pm and ended the same time one day later. I called it the "longest night" as dew fell on everything. We drank hot broth which helped to fight the cold and dampness. My special horse liniment kept my legs working. The university locked the rest rooms at midnight so we ran to the nearby shrubbery. I had run over 109 miles since landing at

Memphis. At the airport when leaving, the race director Gerry Vannoy, handed me a t shirt that read the irrevalent words "marathoners keep it up longer."

The year 1981 was an epic year for the "Huck." Three days prior to the Boston marathon I celebrated the victory over the previous year 104.8 mile protest run. 4/17-20/1981 I decided to run a 205 mile victory run from Albany, New "York to Boston, Massachusetts over the exhausting rough and steep Berkshire mountains. I called it my "A" to "B:" victory ultra for the senior citizens. The last leg of the run was the Boston marathon the police threw me out at near the finish line, the Rosie Rusiz hoax had them on the alert. They chased me but couldn't catch me, so I jumped over the fence and disappeared in the Crowd to the cheers of the thousands of spectators anxiously waiting for some drama while patiently awaiting the winner.

July 5th 1981 I ran "The North Pole Marathon." A frozen race over the frozen tundra and icebergs for 52.2 miles. It made the Boston marathon look like a "Billiard table."

After training for nearly 3 months in a frozen food locker, I ran the Midnight sun ultra marathon. Starting from the Eskimo village of Nanivsivik to Arctic bay—over 2,000 miles north of Montreal—over 500 miles north of the Arctic circle near the north magnetic pole. A helicopter was part of the equipment to scare away unfriendly polar bears. It flew back once and got a new pair inflated sneakers when I blew a pair out on a sharp rock. I was so close to the north pole that my wrist compass hand rotated around in a circle! Once a seal came out of the water and honked at me as if it wondered why I was there. It was over an 11 hour run!

November 21-22, 1981 I went all out to set a 100 mile, 24 hour, age 60 plus record; perhaps a world record. Race certifiers officially and accurately measured and timed the run on an indoor Olympic track. I ran nonstop for 24 hours, a distance of 101 miles 753 yards passing the 100 mile mark in 23:38:07.56 for another record. Little doubt these records have been broken in the years since I then. The indoor race was named the 1981 Marion Corrigan memorial, 24 hour super run in Auburn, New York. The race was held indoors because of snow storm.

A 27 year old lady named Sue Kahler ran 116 miles 676 yards to set national record and number 4th in world category.

The race was won by Al Hastings age 36, he ran 122 miles 528 yards. A detailed description of the entire mind boggling event will be found later in this book.

June 1982 I ran for 3 days and 10 hours in a 6 day race where I was denied official status. I covered on the quarter mile track as recorded 205 miles before I was thrown out by race officials for illegal entry.

In October 4th 1982 in Chicago, Illinois I ran the American Medical Joggers association 50 mile and 100 km certified course set the road runners club of America (NRCA) championship for his time of 10:27:15 for 50 miles and 13:30:20 for the 100km (62.2 miles) American national Championship. The course was a 10 mile loop along the coast of Lake Michigan. I won the record in my age group of over 60 years of age.

October 21-24, 1982 I was just getting warmed up I got an idea of running the entire length of Long Island then over the Verrazano bridge to the start of the New York marathon then turned around and ran the NY city 5 boroughs marathon, starting two hours before the official start. Did I ever get some well deserved attention. There must have been several million spectators screaming and rooting for me thinking that I was the leader. When I told them I had run 160 plus miles from Montauk lighthouse on the tip of Long Island in which the New York Times called a "running odyssey" the stunt was better than winning the NYC marathon it "blew their minds" one news paper called him Evil Knevil of the modern running mania. God must have heard my prayers. Jim Fix now deceased, spoke the immortal words that running was not a religion, a sweaty warm up suit was not a surplice (priest robe), the Verrazzano bridge was not a catherdral and gatoraid (electrolyte replacement glucose) ERG is not communion wine.

I had known since child hood that there was a creator that it didn't make sinse that nothing could become something. Even Albert Einstein after discovering that energy was mass time speed of light squared, came to the same conclusion. Yet daily the world best scientist labour with this conundrum.

I know there is a Creator and His son and Holy Spirit who is a friend of and comforts me in my most trying moments. Yes there is a Heaven because I was clinically dead and got a glimpse of it. There has been many times in my life that God has intervened to protect my life so that I may be a witness personally. True I hear that still small voice strengthening my faith and lowering my fear. In the innate and inner parts of my mind He speaks to me and I truly trust Him. But if you and me don't resist the Devil the devil will not flee (run away).

The bible indicates if we want it to happen we have got to write it down. At age 90 the Creator has always listened to my prayers and done an excellent job in thus far answered those he approved of. My advice to everyone is to get a prayer closet and use it.

1982 the 3rd of October, I ran the New York Canandaigua Lake Ultra marathon. The race was a 60 km run around Canandaigua lake one of the five finger lakes named after one of the five tribes of the Iroquois Indian nation. The name of the race was "Canandaigua Lake Fall Classic." It was a run for financial support for the American Cancer Society. A charity fund raiser. The nickname for the race was "a devil of a good run" and true to its name that was just what it was. Of the many ultra marathons I ever ran, this was the most enjoyable except perhaps the historic Erie Canal run in the following month. It is impossible in this brief summery to even remotely describe this awe-inspiring race in which full details are covered in a chapter 16 found in this book. Please read it, you will love it….For certain God did!

1982 on November 7, I ran my beloved "Erie Canal Run" 60km (37.3 miles) read the chapter in this book, a summary of the famous canal will enlighten you as to the historic significance this canal had upon the development of our country and how the men, immigrants most from Ireland achieved the impossible. If you missed the full story, read it as I mediated upon it in my 60 km ultra marathon in profound amazement. For a detailed and educational review of the construction and operation of the Erie Canal, just read all about it in chapter 17 of this book.

On May 15, 1983 "The Incredible Huck's" heart faltered about a hundred yards short of the finish line while running the Ottawa Canada international marathon at Ottawa, Canada. Two nurses passing by saw my feet sticking out of a ditch and found me with no heart beat and not breathing. Clinically dead they administered CPR to no avail. And lucky for me a team of paramedics stopped and applied their 10,000 volt 2.5 ampere defribulator paddles to my chest. Using a defribulator plus God's grace saved my life. My running career was over. I awoke in the Ottawa hospital after having the oxygen plug removed. After waking, I saw the nurses in pink dresses not white dresses, not Angels I told myself for if so I thought, "I would be looking for wings."

I found my glimpse of Heaven to be or look like a beautiful kaleidoscope panorama. While looking out the hospital window, I saw the beautiful Canada landscape. I heard God's voice tell me, "John you are an old man, give ME praise." Use that other talent I gave you, rather than pounding the pavement with your feet, give ME praise. Use the other gift I gave you, Caress the canvas with a brush."

My amazing career change is truly an astounding self actualization to fulfill God's PROMISE. As shown in subsequent chapters of this book…For the PROVISION…

I lived in spite of losing a coronary artery which altered the lower half of my heart muscle to scar tissue. The remaining two coronary arteries became plugged up ten years later in 1993. I was besieged with excruciating angina pain and was rushed to Albany, NY medical center for bi pass surgery. The surgeons replaced my two coronary arteries with the ones they harvested from my left leg. In April 2001 my heart again faltered, I was outfitted with a pacemaker/defribulator which became inoperative when a condenser shorted out the battery and the manufacturer had a recall. I wondered if it was made by Ford. The medical center installed a new pacemaker/defribulator in 2006 and is operating excellent at my current age. A. Housman wrote, "O moon of my delight that knows to wain how many times will you look for me in this same garden—all in vain?"

One week prior to my heart failure at Ottawa I could tell there was something wrong with my body. The Canandaigua and Erie Canal ultra marathons were causing me to develop slight angina pains as I ran a 10km race held at Canandaigua, NY in my honor by the American cancer society which took me a long 58.30 to finish. As recorded in my running log dated Sunday May 8, 1983 I experienced angina pains severely at the quarter mile marker. I failed to take heed and take a medical stress test to show the condition of my heart. This was just one week to the day before I fell clinically dead at the Ottawa International marathon in Ottawa, Canada near the 26 mile mark, attempting to break the three and half hour limit, and would have except for a heart failure with only 365 yards to go.

I would call after my last breath on this earth "crossing the finish line in heaven." Following Jesus is the greatest heart run. In my 9 years of running with Christ as my copilot there have been hurdles but I have jumped over them with his help. Running with Jesus has great rewards. When I finish life's race and cross the finish line in Heaven and see and hear the screaming angels cheer, and Jesus put a golden crown upon my head I'll give him praise and thanks.

CHAPTER 8

"The Athens International Peace Marathon"

Memories of a classic race. The Athens international peace marathon, a standard 26.2 mile marathon which started at the village of marathon, Greece and ended at the giant 31,000 seat stadium in Athens, Greece; on the 22nd of April 1979.

The race director Mr. Steven W. Whitehead also the organizer joined our flight to Athens which turned out to take about 16 hours of flight time. Upon arrival we were bused to the hotel Alexandria plush accommodation in downtown Athens. There we unwound and began our sightseeing tours. Betty, my wife made our program. The first day we went to local sightseeing events, next day to Neptune's Temple at Sounion. The following day to Delphi and the day before the race to Delphi to see the oracle. We also visited the Parthanon and Acropolis along with the Athens museum. The day following the race we went on a cruise to Aegina, Poros, and Hyrda. Syronic islands of the bay of Athens. They took a great place in the Greek independence of 1821. The thing I remember most was riding on a donkey.

The day before the race we made a short tour of the race course. It was nice to hear the Greeks talk again for it had been over twenty years since sailing as a radio officer on a Greek ship for two and a half years in the merchant marine. The language hadn't changed. Many of our words have been taken from theirs.

The origin of Athens began in the Neolithic age so the story goes when Neptune struck the Acropolis with his trident and water and a fiery steed sprang forth, however the gods in judgment gave the city to Athena "Goddess of Wisdom" for her gift an olive branch signifying peace and prosperity.

King Diarus had captured for Persia the known world of that day, except for tiny Greece. After a futile attempt he later led his vast army himself. The runner Pheidippides ran to Sparta for help, he received none, ran back to Marathon and joined the Greeks in fight, and upon victory ran over twenty miles to Athens in utter exhaustion only to mutter the words "rejoice we conquer" and died. He had to carry a torch all night to see with. The message told the General in Athens it was not required to pull an amphibious landing behind the Persians.

Enough for history, the time for us to run the sacred course was at hand. My nose was so plugged by carbon monoxide that it was necessary to use an inhaler to breathe. At the gun the lead runners leaped forward, however my pace was much slower. My intentions were to run 52.4 miles further than they. My main objective was to get into the Guinness book of world records for running it three times back to back nonstop in under 16 hours.

The marathon run turned out to be very interesting. About four miles out we run through an olive grove that marked the location of the battlefield where the Persians and Greeks fought at the battle of Marathon. There were some ladies who handed out olive branches in honor of Athena goddess founder of Athens. We stuck them in our head bands and ran inspired. My wife manned the 20 mile water station, a young runner had stopped there to rest and I talked him into running with me to finish. A runner ahead of us had been grazed by a car and the driver followed him to the finish line and offered his daughter's hand as a dowry…the year before a lady came looking for her son and found him just running to finish, she jumped in and chased him to the finish line…yelling Stephanos, Stephano's, Stephano's!

The runner I was talking to in an effort to get him to finish was taking more time than expected but he struggled along. Finally there it was! The stadium. We looked like stragglers. My running partner looked like an emotionally paralyzed jogger. My time was off, it took a bit over five hours, my worst time yet. The crowd yelled "here comes The Incredible Huck" even though I didn't feel so good about it. However the runner I'd helped would perhaps remember that run the rest of his life. There wasn't much beer left though. I just turned around and announced that I was going to run back to our start line and be back at around midnight, and told my wife to meet me when I phoned her at the hotel.

The return trip to the village of Marathon was much more exciting. The temperature was now in the high eighties. Sweat was running down my nose. My Greek language now became important. As I ran through the city of Athens people began to ask me questions. One little boy held up his ice cream cone and said, "Trofagis" translated means "you eat," did I ever! It was the best ice cream I'd ever tasted and I yelled to him "Efkaristo" (thank you). On and on I ran now out in the counry. Suddenly I heard some loud music and Greek being sung…"argapimani mu, argapimani su" (I love you, you love me). Well, I stopped and walked over to the big party which turned out to be a wedding. They were astounded that an American could converse with them, they had me dancing around and drinking a big glass of ouiso, a liquorice tasting alcoholic drink. Before long the stuff hit me and I cleared out, it was really potent. After saying "haratay" (good bye) I took off in a run towards Marathon. Dancing around in a squat had limbered me up. My calculation as my watch showed me I was about half way to Marathon, running steady and jogging every fifteen minutes to rest from the hot sun was working. My return trip was proving to be more interesting. Before long I saw a spur road leading up to of all things, an American military base. It was close and it looked as a perfect place as any to get water. The Greek booze had worn off and taking care of my thirst was first order. The air force troops treated me good and were joyful to hear my crazy story and kept shaking their heads as the story unrolled. To keep on schedule I had to get to Marathon by seven o'clock and get water at a little store nearby. The sun was sinking and I'd be running in the dark on the narrow road back to Athens. Now it was becoming easier because the afternoon heat wacked me good. There came a gentle breeze and my spirit picked up about 9:30. I'd reached the half way mark, the little spiti (house) where the wedding took place nearly five hours ago. They had moved there celebration indoors. But were still playing music. I thought they would still be whooping it up all night.

    I should be able to make it back to the stadium in the remaining two and a half hours to get there by midnight. The traffic was heavy now near the outskirts of Athens. My nose told me so because it was becoming burned by fumes and my eyes started watering, little cars zoomed around, those Greeks never stop running those little cars around. They can drive many miles per gallon. Gasoline cost then in 1979 over three dollars per gallon. Closing in on the stadium near eleven thirty and I had three miles about to go. I just needed to keep up a ten minute pace. I was very happy to see the stadium after getting to the finish line. I walked back around the corner and found a small café where I phoned Betty at the Alexander hotel, she grabbed a cab and met me there for a coffee.

The following day Betty and myself went on a cruise ship to the Greek islands of Poros, Hydra and the guided trips gave us a good understanding of Greek history. We got full disclosure on Delphi. 180 kms from Athens in northwest direction. It stands if isolated from the rest of the world, like an amplitheatre across the semi circle formed by the Phaedriades, two big lumps of rocks encompassing the valley Mt. Kirphis stands behind and the light falls on two red cliffs—the rodini and flambouko many reflections follow each other endlessly. Long before Apollo the son of Zeus other deities worshiped there, including earth goddess Gea, Themis, Demeter and Poseidon (Neptune) Python, and Gea's son Pyton guarded the oracle and for some time the whole area was called Pytho. Dorian crete guarded it. Out of the struggle of Apollow with Python a new god created, Pythius. As the Pythian oricle reputation grew it became a cultural and athelitic meeting ground. Many countries brought votive offerings to the oracle. Ancient Greeks believed that Delphi was the point where earth touched the divine: The navel of the earth. Where two eagles had come together when Zeus let them fly in opposite directions. Greek Philosophers wrote on the walls "know thyself" and "Avoid excess." Art flourished in Delphi. Pythis is no longer there to make prophesies, nor does the oracle predict the future anymore but you can take in the spirit by strolling through the sacred grounds…

    I climed up to the seat where the oracle sat and sat on her rock seat. Closed my eyes and dreamed for a couple of minutes a powerful soul revealing power came over me and my prayer was answered, a voice spoke and I heard it say "you will run the race of Pheidippides three times back to back to back." It was weird. Thanks to my wife Betty, I'd seen a lot of the culture that Greece has to offer and remembered back to the many stories the Greek sailors had told me during my stay with them. They were eager to learn the English language and as I became more proficient. I was able to teach them enough words and sentences to get by.

    It seemed sort of sad meeting in the lobby of the hotel Alexanderia with all the chatter going on, runners rehasing their historic run. I was doing some serious thinking. One of the fellows and his assistant had come along to make a movie of the run. Mike, the public relations man, contacted me and asked if I would like to capitalize on my stunts? My answer was "why not." Mike said he would give me an outline for a good running book and while in Greece he had filmed a great deal of footage of many crazy and interesting things that were news worthy. Mike promised that upon returning to the USA he would send me a legal contract. Strange enough, he kept his word. We hooked up and gave it a try, not much money but a lot of running shoes, vitamins, t shirts of which I already had a couple of hundred. In fact when I made a short film for pm magazine at the Syracuse carrier dome, they hung the marathon t shirts on a line and they reached all way across the dome which is over 150 feet! Several radio and tv stations gave me lots of coverage but little cash, Peugeot bicycles gave me some super bike uniforms, shoes and a bike helmet. All the vitamin company went wild when finding an old man who ran marathons and ultra marathons and all sorts of unheard of races. I'd developed into a household word.

CHAPTER 9

"The Ultimate Challenge"

My wife Betty, who is also my handler, and I arrived a week prior to the start of the western states 100 mile endurance run at Squaw valley inn, the home of the 1960 winter Olympics. We'd flown out to Sacramento and were welcomed by my crew Ray Kelly, his wife Marian, and their niece Christie, from Rancho Cordovia nearby. My crew along with their French poodle, Pierre, lived at our resort park in Lee center, New York for several years. He had worked in the same communications area with me at Griffith Air force base and later moved to Mather air force base near Rancho Cordovia where he took on the duties of a wire chief for the base.

Ray took us up to Squaw Valley the next day after a night out at Epphies restaurant that sponsored "The Great Race," a relay with runner, canoe and bicycle combination. We worked out all the logistics for the race and his niece Christie joined the support crew. Ray would use his Chevy pickup truck to carry the essential items, food, flashlights, clothing, vitamins, horse liniment (analgesic), energy bars, first aid items, etc. He charted the back roads which he knew quite well from working with the Bell telephone company years ago. He'd snow shoed the area and had a good knowledge of the trails. I was truly fortunate to have such a good support team. At Squaw Valley I started training in earnest for the race. For three days I ran up to the peak at Emigrant pass, about 9,000 feet high, following the trail up ski slopes and over mountainous terrain. About the only food we could find at the lodge was pizza which raised my triglyceride level to 220/mg/dl which meant there was a lot of blood fat to use and metabolize for the run.

The depletion run was as vivid as the 100 miler. That Wednesday morning I gulped down my vitamins after looking over a large selection; I chose some B-15, potent calcium panganate from Russia, even the price was super, I looked at the $15.95 price stamped on the bottle cap and thought.... Here goes 32 cents as I popped two of the aspirin looking tablets. My eye caught sight of the big bottle of Vitamin C, time release capsules, they were like huge horse pills...a full gram and a half of asboric acid. I gulped down a couple of them with an orange juice chaser. I chewed up some 400 I.U. Vitamin E capsules with selenium for quick synergistic reaction. They are oily tasting like fish oil. Then I grabbed a bottle of calcium and magnesium chewables and crunched on the dolomite, egg shell, oyster shell in the gravely tasting things...it's hard to disguise either constituent as they neither taste pleasant. Then, I went on a binge: 200 IUs of Vitamin D, Folic Acid, PAB, a multiple vitamin, B complex, bioten, RNA/DNA, potassium, sodium alginate, beef liver, niacinamide, lechithin, kelp, B-12, B6, cider vinegar, choline inositol, and a garlic parsley (which always never failed to give me terrible sour burps), plus some chelated iron, bee pollen, oil of primrose, chelated copper, organic selenium, zinc, vita—lea and manganese tablets. And as a kicker I threw in a powerful stress complex, and elongated pill that super charged me to the extent I felt like a race horse in the starting gates!

Armed with all those ergonenic aids and a couple cups of black coffee to metabolize my body fats and triglycerides, I ran one of the most unforgettable depletion runs of my life. It was Wednesday morning and in three days prior I'd run to the top of Emigrant Peak to get acclimated. But, today, I was going to run about 15 miles to Truckee, a town North of Squaw Valley. My wife was taking the greyhound bus to Truckee so I decided to run the 15 miles in two hours and try to get there first as Betty would arrive around noon. That meant I'd have to run a 7 1/2 mph pace. The road was nearly flat, with some curves, glancing over my shoulder the three huge mountains started fading. I could see well, 8800 foot DT22, Elmigrant Peak and Granite Chief as they became part of the background along route 80. There were creeks, campgrounds and homes beyond the reach of even the wealthy. Faster my feet seemed to run, it was like I was flying. My hamstrings moved me almost effortlessly, like perpetual motion. I tried to get rid of the last traces of glycogen in my muscles. My spirits really jumped when reading the road sign Truckee. Suddenly there was a giant sooshh and the bus passed me. Betty waved frantically from the rear window, amazed that I'd run so far…I threw both hands up and waved furiously, then went into a sprint as the suction pushed me toward the ditch. Running with renewed vigor, I reached downtown Truckee about 5 minutes later and found Betty shopping in a health food store. She had purchased all the dried fruit and bananas for my loading phase. I felt like a giant sponge which had been squeezed and wrung so tight when it let go I'd take on a double supply of glycogen. Even my ADT fibers were twitching for phosphates.

It was the 4th of July and Betty and I took a tour around Lake Tahoe, about a 72 mile trip. The bus stopped in Tahoe city and Betty put a few dollars in the slot machine and just as the bus was ready to pull out she hit the jackpot; bing, bing, bing. Quarters started pouring out of the one armed bandit, she crammed in all the quarters she could get into her purse and I grabbed both hands full and we ran to the bus, but that machine was still spilling them all over the floor, even after we left.

Each moment the suspense grew. Jim Kerse from New Zealand came to see me. We'd run the Phildippides marathon in Athens, Greece about 5 weeks earlier: only I went on to run the course. More than 78.6 miles as a training run for the race at hand. Ray Million from Oklahoma visited me also. He'd just did some running in the Grand Canyon down in Arizona and screwed up his ankles. Jim and Ray were psyched up as other runners arrived and the anxiety grew. A wrestling team from San Francisco composed of young kids showed up also, one of them was a Chinese boy and he did some running and was very happy to run a six mile training run with me that Thursday morning. Betty enjoyed the large swimming pool and would have liked to swim in the large Olympic one where they were training the Olympic swimmers, but they were under heavy security. We stayed in a cabin at Squaw Valley Inn which was constructed by the CCC workers back in the mid thirties.

Thursday morning Ray and Marian arrived to take us back to Sacramento where I was to meet my PR man, Mike Hartfield, from Portland. He had made arrangements for me to meet the press and TV at the Red Lion Motor Inn in Sacramento. We went by way of South Tahoe City where Betty managed to get rid of the quarters she had won the day before at Harrah's and Harolds casinos. I had enough left to "pig out" on some super carbos at the clubs dining room on the top floor. I undid 6 months of hard Olympic type training in a half hour in that place, plus put on an extra handicap by at least 5 pounds. (Note: years later the 5th floor was blown out when trying to defuse a time bomb that exploded by robbers demanding random)

Mike, his wife Wanda, and their two sons, Darien and Tristan were waiting at the Red Lion Inn, and he had the press conference all set up. At 10:00 in the morning two television crews and some newsmen including the sports editor, Don Bloom, from the Sacramento Union attended the press conference. The Sacramento Union gave me a big splash and likewise the TV.

Mike, his family, Betty and I rode in their Mercedes back to Squaw Valley, where we were to be weighed in and briefed on the trail. I gave the support truck my little plastic bag of supplies to deliver at the checkpoints where my support crew couldn't get to. Kelly and my support crew were busy getting all the logistic problems solved and loading their pickup truck. I wouldn't see them until Robinson Flat at 2:30 the next day.

I awoke at 3:00 a.m. that Saturday morning, July 7, 1979. I thought it would be the most important day in my life. My wife Betty had also heard the little alarm clock that had a voice like a fire bell, and didn't seem to share my enthusiasm at that time of morning. She started pumping out some negative thoughts, like all the thousands of dollars I'd squandered in the last 6 years, and that runners were all mental cases. I changed stations quick before reality had a chance to psyche me out and drug her out of bed while she was still ranting something like mentally freaked out, and she was not going to give my psychiatrist anymore money and I could go more crazy, etc. I tried to console her with the exciting news that there were pancakes for us in the Olympic house, but that didn't help much. After putting on warm up suits, we stumbled through the darkness to the Squaw Valley Lodge. It was almost a midnight breakfast of pancakes. I carried my own fructose syrup so as not to kick up my insulin and wipe out my glycogen in my muscles. I drank a large glass of milk because Dr. Lang, race director, said it would cause the ADT molecules to drink up more glycogen as the phosphates would cause them to "twitch." I went along with it, I needed all the help I could get from those biochemists.

At 4:00 am I returned to the cabin and made preparations for an event now only an hour away. Looking at my feet I noticed that every toe nail was black and some missing toe nails from the 78.6 mile run a few weeks earlier in Athens. I took a big jar of Cramer skin lube, a viscous green grease and put a big glob on my toes, heels, groin, chest and armpits. Then turned my socks wrong side out so the fuzz would keep small rocks out of my shoes; and I can plainly remember all the details of putting on my Bill Rodgers "singlet" and sub 4 dark blue running shorts. Then I pinned on a plastic sandwich baggie in which was a snake bite kit, six fructose tablets, some dolomite and a zinc tablet, plus 4 caffeine tablets and some green vita-lea pills. It would take several pages to describe their contents. It was what I called "an external colostomy bag." I also carried a high protein energy bar, rich in fructose and vitamins and I also had them in my logistic bags at the checkpoints. I knew they would get me to Hodgson's cabin 10.4 miles away.

I looked at those formidable mountains in front of me totally obscured by the blackness of night. We lined up in the Squaw Valley parking lot, about 143 "crazies" toed the line. I thought then about what the electro cardiologist said to me nearly 6 years ago, "see your lawyer and make out your will and if you are still alive, then see your doctor." That was 6 years ago. Maybe I'd get a trophy or a $6.00 belt buckle or a plaque, or be eaten up by a grizzly bear. There wasn't any money in it; a little shamateurism, at the most. The temperature was only a few degrees above freezing at the start of the race, and hovering in the low twenties near the top of Emigrant pass, nearly 9,000 feet in the Sierra Nevada Mountains only 5 miles ahead.

Dr. Lind said, "its 5:00 a.m., Go" and suddenly everyone was running through the early morning darkness. Beside me was Cowman Shirk, we shook hands and I lost him on the first big grade about half a mile from the start. The Cowman gave an eerie yodel that resounded off the mountain sides and echoed back. I'll always remember Cowman; he had a long bushy beard, kind heart and legs like steel. Weighing about 200 pounds he was running more like a billy goat than a cow. He wore a head dress with horns on it. Once he let me put it on and I gave out a big MOOOO. That was after we'd run the Hawaiian Triathlon, biked and swam for 140.6 miles six months later. The Cowman won the WS100 in 1976 and was the only one finished that year in 24:30.

I'd run to the top of Emigrant pass three times in the last week in training runs and knew it would take me at least 80 minutes to go that first 5 miles. I just kept looking for those yellow ribbons in the old pine trees. I was choking on the dust, and dipping up water from the mountain streams along the way. There was a 30% reduction in oxygen at that level, and I ran past the cables of the ski tows eager to reach Emigrant pass where I'd put the American flag two days earlier in a rock tower. My breath was just short of an anaerobic limit and I had reached the crusty ice and crunchy snow region near the pass. An old runner, 65 year old Boris Yankoff was burning the course. He beat me to the top of the Emigrant Mountain, but I caught him at Hodgson's cabin. He looked beat and dropped out at Robinson flat. John Arberry ran with me from the top of Emigrant pass to Hodgson's cabin, but pulled away just before Red Star ridge. I didn't catch up with him until just before entering Forest hill at 70 miles out. The view from Emigrant pass was breath taking. To the North the blue waters of Donner Lake twelve miles away looked close, and to the rear 5 miles to the foot of the hill was Squaw Valley. It lay like a view from the window of a jet flying at about 10,000 feet. Just variegated tinges of green, sparkling needle thin streams, and the buildings that were a tiny brownish spec or two. It appeared as an ancient Utopia lying peaceful in the Emerald Valley bespeckled with tints of vitreous colored hues mingled with cobalt and Prussian blue chromas. Ahead lay the first downhill decent about a mile and then it took a sudden upturn and then about another 1500 feet drop to Hodgson's cabin where we first saw any aid or support, the first drink. I popped a few more fructose pills to make it up to Foresthill Divide, about 15 miles out from the start. It was a level stretch that ran for 16 miles without water. I drank two small squirt bottles I'd bought in Athens for the Pheidippides run in the near 100 degree weather. Then came the torturous decent into Duncan canyon, the flexors took, It was at one hell of a beating on that decent, another 1500 feet of slip sliding down hill. I recall a big round rock which resembled a cannon ball tumbling about four feet down the steep incline and smashing my right heal. It made me yelp and scream which reverberated up and down the canyon walls. I'd removed my windbreaker and tied it around my waist to leave with Kelly at the next stop at Robinson Flat. That big rock had done some damage to my right heel. Suddenly I thought about the greatest Greek warrior and his vulnerable heel. Achilles hero of Homer's Iliad, killed when Paris wounded him in the heel, which was also his one vulnerable spot. I had to resort to metaphysical healing for the pain, after contracting my inner mind and applying a lot of positive thinking, it acted like a faith healer. I was asking all the Saints in Heaven to intercede, especially St. Jude for hopeless cases, as mine seemed to be now. By now the numbness had disconnected my mind from my body and by the time I'd reached Robinson Flat my stride was all screwed up. I was all hunched over like I had a bad case of scoliosis, curvature of the spine.

At Robinson flat, Dr. Lind checked my weight and I'd lost only 4 pounds as I managed to drink from earlier streams and the quirt bottles. It was wonderful to see Ray and Christie with the old black Chevy and cold orange juice. He took a quick picture and I wolfed down a banana and hit the trail. They were going to meet me at last chance and give me a flashlight as it would be dark before reaching Michigan Bluff. Leaving Robinson Flat about 35 miles out, I ran down steep canyon walls to the last chance checkpoint and aid station at about 50 miles, the half way point. This part of the trail was filled with soft silty dust, mixed with a lot of horse manure. I could sympathize with the first runner to do this insane run, Gordy Ainsleigh, who ran against 190 horses and came in 45th place.

It was at last chance that I met up with the twins, Karen and Peggy Stok from Redwood City, California. They left about 4 minutes before me, as I had developed a huge blister on my foot just above the ankle bone where the heel counter in my Nike LDV's kept digging in when my foot would pronate inwards in the rounded dust filled trail. The first aid man put a round rubber donut pad on it after swabbing it with antiseptic. It felt real good and I left in pursuit of the twins and caught up with them on the steep descent into the north middle fork of American river and I ran up the unbelievable incline, but Peggy couldn't make it past the river. I believe she had hypoglycemia, low blood sugar and leg cramps. Her sister Karen took care of her while I ran ahead and alerted the first aid crew at Devil thumb, and waited for Karen as she had a flashlight and darkness had set in. The medical group took care of Peggy while Karen and I ran down the steep hill into El Dorando Canyon at about 60 miles out. I ran ahead with her flashlight and she followed in my footsteps. She had saved me from failure and I'll always be grateful to her for that. About a half mile from Michigan Bluff some rangers patrolling the trail told us to hurry it up that two 400 pound black bears had just crossed the trail 200 yards ahead of us and some rattle snakes were crawling around in the moonlight. That put a shot of adrenalin in us, in fact Karin started really kicking in that mile. She ran away from me holding the flashlight and the moon was bright and she could see quite far, enough so as not to stumble over any boulders or trip on tree roots. Karen beat me to Michigan bluff by 3 minutes; she could have won the race if those bears had not crossed her path up Emigrant Mountain.

I was very glad to see Kelly and Christie. They had my flashlights and orange juice, a double handful of vitamins, and some horse liniment called Banalog, it took most of the tightness out of my legs and my stride returned to normal. Karen learned Peggy was ok. She left Michigan bluff two minutes after I did. She had found a pacer to try and pick up some lost time. they passed me on a steep hill just before Volcano Canyon. I had got lost by following some runner's shoe tracks; later found out that it was Lono Tyson from Morovia, California. I was about 4 miles, two out and back and I couldn't understand why there were no yellow ribbons, yet those shoe tracks just kept going along a trail, but then suddenly they hit a dead end and just turned around so I followed them back to the main trail. This kind of thing is really upsetting and only the word "pissed" seemed to express just what I felt over that bad break. This would no doubt cost me the last part of the race but the pace I held would just about get me there, if nothing else went wrong.

I'd picked up my red windbreaker at Michigan bluff and it felt good to have it since the chill of the midnight air made my teeth chatter. Kelly said he'd meet me in Foresthill, the 70 mile point, where the trail went onto a highway and through town. The winds picked up and bent the giant pine trees at which point I began to wonder if I'd completely ignored the realms of sanity as I ate the WS100 bullet and almost stepped on a rattle snake twice. The snowballing lunacy with which I started yesterday morning was overshadowed by intelligent fatigue, but again my mind would not let me quit or feel the full blunt of fatigue and pain. Old age was surely catching up with me at this rate. I got free of these doldrums by re-generating my body with caffeine tablets to metabolize some of the fatty acids in my blood stream, as I was burning fat at this point and the glycogen reserves were long depleted and I knew the blood sugar was way down, making coherence difficult. This was a lonely wilderness where every wild animal sniffed at my footsteps. Then as my blood sugar became dangerously low, my mind started hallucinating. My early childhood flashed upon the panoramic screen in my mind with startling realness. I remember plainly seeing the antiquated broken down sharecropper farm with its dilapidated barn and rusty windmill, our home, a shed like structure with a tin roof. I recall even the trees in the front yard, those threadbare mesquite, scrub post oak, sage brush and black jacks. My mind still kept playing tricks. There I was in a thunderstorm and running to the dugout in the back yard with Pa, Ma, my sister Edna and brother Basil to escape a tornado. It was all so memorable, Pa driving me over the rough country roads telling me about the battle of Marathon, Pheidippides and looking down at my tiny legs wondering then who or how anyone could run for 26 miles. It seems I'd gone back 55 years in time. There out in the Texas prairie chasing jack rabbits, coyotes, sage hens and road runners. There were some cages out in the back yard. If the birds or animals were small enough, I would catch one once in a while and keep it a day or two and then turn it loose to run after another day. It was my first trophy case.

Up and up I climbed for over 1,500 feet and started descending into Volcano Canyon, then up another thousand feet to Foresthill where I again became dumbfounded by the full moon causing an ever series of highlights on the blackness of the landscape. Time and time again the shimmering gossamers and radians reflected from the heavens above and fell upon the mountain trail as I ran. It was surely the world's toughest footrace and the challenge grew greater, my every thought became that to finish as I jumped from boulder to boulder like a mountain goat. The mountain was like a sea of rocks, the battery in my bionic legs was getting weaker; the many cases of pneumonia during my life had eaten away parts of my lungs and their anaerobic capability was just about at its limit. I thought for a while about who was up front and who had won the race. This was surely the trail to infinity, the culmination of inconceivable pain, the sigma of bleakness, the sum total of loneliness, the apex of desolation. Yet the beauty of the trees silhouetted by the moon wooed my bent brain like heaven drags upon the roots of hell. That moon of delight casting those eerie sivery shadows on the trail added to moments a treasury of memories. Mental souvenirs never to be forgotten. How my thoughts skipped, danced and went wild in heartfelt joy. That night alone with only the sincere warmth of my thoughts, perhaps the moon is still looking for me along that trail, all in vain.Mike Catlin, Davis CA won race.

Up ahead a man walking in the darkness with a flashlight and a thin light lit us the road in front of him. I was on a highway. A macadam road approaching Foresthill village, it must have been sometime around 2:00am Sunday morning. I slowed down as I passed him and how surprised I was to see it was John Arberry. The guy had left me at Red Star Bridge at the 26 mile mark. He was muttering incoherently and his body was still going but he had become irrational and disorientated and said they were going to pull him off the course at Michigan Bluff, but he talked them out of it. We met Kelly and Christie about 3 miles down the road in the village of Foresthill. We drank some orange juice I popped a handful of vitamin pills and ate a banana. Then resupplied my plastic support bag that was pinned to my shorts. Then I gulped down a cup of Sweet lite liquid natural sweetener, that really perked me up, along with a no-doze tablet. John and I ran all the way to White Oak flat where Kelly and Christie were waiting for us. He gave me a pair of shoes to ford the Middle Fork of the American River. We ran wonderfully those 8 miles, it was a 2,000 foot drop but after White Oak Flat about 2 miles from the main bar crossing at 82 miles out, John could no longer keep up with me. I told him I had to pick up the pace when a fellow riding a horse said our pace was too slow to finish under 30 hours. It was then I became irrational when the thoughts of not finishing drove me into a frenzied, emotional state and caused me to push with every vestage of remaining energy. Over cobblestones to the river where I changed shoes and swam across it dragging my sore limbs through the icy water for about 220 yards.

    The sun rose like a big fried egg and turned into a blaze of forge like embers. I continued to run like a demon. I passed two other runners including Karen Stok. All that was in my mind was the $11,500 I'd spent over the years on the running gambit, plus the PR man and the $50.00 entry fee. It was not too difficult to work myself into a dither having spent this amount and gone to so much bother to achieve this point so near success. Well I was not going to blow it. I charged those hills like a kamikaze pilot screaming kill, kill, kill. I paid for this emotional outbreak because when I hit highway 49 at the 92.7 mile mark my hamstrings began to tighten up. I rubbed on some more Banalog and limped along for a few minutes and they came alive on the hills leading up to Pointed Rocks Ranch at the 95 mile mark. Then I could see the big suspension bridge. I was going to make it to "No Hands Bridge." At 97 miles out, I thought it was a downhill stretch. My legs were beat on this 1,000 foot downhill run in about a mile. Digging my feet into the trail to keep from falling forward was pure torture. After seeming like an eternity, I arrived at No Hands Bridge. My wife Betty, Mike my PR man along with his family, Kelly and Christie were all waiting. I continued across the bridge on the heals of Jim Shea from Loomis California, who finished about 5 minutes before I did, and Richard Collins of Oakland California about 14 miles ahead of me. But Karen Stok was not in sight. I'd told her when I passed a few miles back to hurry and hoped she and her pacer had followed my suggestion. There was no time to lose. The drama was building up to where my PR man and Kelly my crew chief were going to kill me if I failed to beat the 30 hours. I ran across the bridge and dipped some water out of a creek alongside it as it trickled through the rocks on the trail. The temperature was in the 90's now and sweat trickled off my nose as I continued to run. Kelly had given me Rosie the Rattler, a toy rattle snake that I was going to attach to my Achilles tendon when crossing the finish line to prove that I was stronger than the greatest Greek god.

    From "No Hands Bridge" to Auburn was 3 miles up a 1,000 foot mountain. This was truly a sadistic course designed for a masochist. I thought as I jogged up that last few feet and reached the highway. Time was running out. I still had a mile to go and only 8 and a half minutes left. This was the Grand Finale, it was now or never. A runner met me who I thought was Andy Gonzales, 1977 and 1978 winner from Colfax California. The runner said "Go for it Huck!" My PR man, Mike had his camera going and it was time to sprint, time to put my mind and body into zones they had never been before, reach deep I told the fellow I thought was Andy. I was ready to kick a 7 minute mile to let everything hangout. They don't call me Incredible Huck for nothing. I ran with the fury of the saints, not wishing to invoke the devil and get tripped up at this point in the race. Suddenly there it was, the entrance to the Auburn Placer High School Stadium. Mike with his two boys and a couple of race officials joined me on the track. This was it, time to burn the course, head back, chin out, give it hell. It was going to be close. This was the ultimate climax as I rounded the last corner and headed into the home stretch. I clenched my fists and grit my teeth so tight that my facial expression resembled that of a Cheshire cat, just like a Jimmy Carter smile. My blood pressure was like a hydraulic ram, hypertension run amuck, everyone was standing and screaming, my wife, Kelly, Christie and Mike. Pictures were snapped of the finish. Dr. Lind took off his hat and brought it down just as I crossed the finish line. I will never forget those timers' words - 29:58:28. I'd become the oldest official runner to ever make the course in under 30 hours. I didn't have time to tie Rosie the rattler to my heal. But wait the crowd was screaming again and there she came, Karen! I ran to meet her as she put on the most furious kick I ever saw would she make it? As her foot crossed the finish line, the timer called out 30 hours. She had become the youngest runner ever to finish the Western states 100 mile endurance run. Kelly handed me a big glass of orange juice, only this time it was the biggest screwdriver I ever saw. I walked back to Kelly's old 1967 pickup truck that would take me to a hot shower and a good meal. That evening, at the awards ceremony, I summed it all up as 6 years of hard training for 30 hours of the hardest work I ever did for a lifetime of memories. Running 100 miles over the High Sierra Nevada Mountains nonstop, with their elevation gain of almost 20,000 feet, is like running up and down the Empire state building about 20 times.

What they had done, what they had seen, heard, felt, feared, the places, the sounds, the colors, the cold, the darkness, the emptiness, the bleakness, the beauty. Til they died, this stream of memory would set them apart, if imperceptibly to anyone but themselves, from anyone else. For they had crossed the mountains....Bernard De Voto

CHAPTER 10

INTERESTING HIGHLIGHTS OF THE TRIATHLON

I left from Syracuse, New York airport at 9:12 a.m. on January 9, 1980 and arrived at Honolulu, T.H. the same day at 7:30 p.m. The plane was delayed for about an hour and a half due to typhoon, hurricane and spin off tornadoes.

I was met at the airport by Mr. Warren McCullom, an engineer with the Army at Honolulu. Warren and his girl friend Kathy took me to a pasta place called the Spaghetti factory, at which point we were met by three other crew members, Bob Kimble, his wife Carol and their friend Karen who worked at the real estate company managed by Carol. She was formerly a cheer leader with the Philadelphia Eagles before moving to Hawaii. Her name was Karen Furlong, a fitness girl who had recently swam the 2.4 mile rough water course, rode her bicycle 112 miles and ran 26.2 mile marathon but on separate days.

To get better acquainted with my crew, I took them to a wine and spaghetti dinner which only came to $27.44 plus $2.56 tip. We all agreed on the course of action. Warren would take my bike to Eki bike shop and have it assembled. The shipping cost was $14.00. The cost to assemble the bike was $39.53. The cost to replace the flat tire was $13.97 (tire and tube). Re-adjust and box for shipment was $9.36. Re-place rear wheel bent during the race, new rim $18.00 and labor was $10.00. Gas and oil for the Toyota truck was $16.00. Miscellaneous expenses of ice, juice, beer was $13.53. Three regular coffees was $1.25.

The next night we took the crew over to an 18th floor penthouse with glass windows on all sides so that the city of Honolulu and Waikiki were plainly visible at night. The owner was Lorrin Lee, a Chinese fellow who taught mind power. I ended up teaching him all about metaphysical healing power.

Warren explained to me how to swim the open seas by visualization of a gold rope attached from a powerful ship to one's head and to think gold when looking down into the depths of the sea while doing the rotation crawl stroke - when the face is in the ocean and air is being exhaled from the lungs. This tip proved to be of big value to me. Mind conditioning is extremely important for the premier endurance event of the world.

I picked up some Chinese food at the Asian Garden. The total cost of dinner for the whole crew was $39.52. I always eat meatless chop suey or chow mein prior to running an ultra marathon as it contains lots of liquids and does not stay in the stomach the day of the race as it contains no solids. Spaghetti was eaten two days prior to the race which helps to build up glycogen in the muscles. I drank a glass of milk so the phosphates would trigger the ADP molecules in the muscle fibers and cause them to twitch and absorb another 90 to 100% additional glycogen, its all very scientific. I was on a full carbohydrate loading program for this event. The severe bronchial infection from the change of climate left me almost completely without a voice, it settled in my larynx and sinuses. I resorted to profound metaphysical healing and held the infection in check at that point, keeping it out of my lungs which would have been disastrous. It would have quickly spread into pneumonia had I not devoted 15 minutes, three times daily talking to my higher self and energized mind. I used every bit of my mind power.

I had run out of B-15, calcium panganate, which also plays a big role in knocking out the flu, of course I took the 31 vitamins and minerals that Thompson supplied me with at no cost. I also took some extra zinc which heals, and iron that builds more red blood corpuscles. I also took 5 grams daily of Vitamin C which is about 2 to 3 grams more than normal.

The Chinese food must have been made with meat stock, I think it must have had pork in it. I am extremely allergic to pork of any kind. It causes the uric acid crystals to form in my big right toe joint and causes very painful gout.

At 3:00 a.m. on Saturday morning (the day of the triathlon), when I awoke, I discovered my right big toe was goutish. It was swollen to the point I could not get on my running shoe. After hopping back into bed from the bathroom on my left foot, I started applying the strongest metaphysical healing I knew, it was reinforced with a special audio visual technique. Within five minutes I had it under control and the swelling began to subside. Normally it take three treatments to get results. I just did not have the time to waste because in only 4 hours I would be starting the 1980 Hawaiian triathlon by plunging in the raging sea and swimming the rough water course for 2.4 miles. It normally takes about three treatments of magnetic mind power to cure strongly resistant illness but my positive mind got me through. I tried again when bicycling but could not concentrate enough as it was extremely dangerous to dissociate my mind for any length of time from my body: it takes absolute concentration to ride a bike over those hazardous roads; full of pot holes and steep shoulders, plus heavy and large vehicle traffic, like buses, trucks and oversized vehicles on a two lane highway. My goutish toe bothered me again at the start of the marathon and I limped during the first ten miles until my mind got rid of it. I am a vegetarian and cannot stand purines of any extent. Foods with high purine counts cause havoc with my big toe joints (hot spots). One attack I had was after a 50 mile 9 1/2 hour run. I completed the race in Allentown Pa., where after running in the rain all day I drank some hot soup with meat stock and my toe swelled up to twice its normal size.

Two days before the Harrisburg marathon in Penna., the doctor in the emergency room at the Rome hospital advised me to go to bed for a week and not run for six weeks. Well, I looked at the toe and turned on the metaphysical healing technique that Evelyn Monahan taught me and inside of one hour I was on my way to Harrisburg (400 miles away). I ran a darn good marathon that day and the next weekend I ran a 50 miler over the Appalachian Mountains called the "Trail To Infinity" - the John F. Kennedy memorial run (50 miles) from Boonsboro, Maryland to St. James, Maryland and a week later the Jersey shore marathon at Asbury Park, New Jersey. This was the first time I had any gout like symptoms since that day. Anyway, I knew how to handle it. I think so positive that my mind has become magnetically orientated with the powers and laws of the universe. You must think positive to run nonstop, as I did, for 30 hours over the Sierra Nevada Mountains. 100 miles with encroaching fatigue, the kind that changes snowballing lunacy to sanity.

During my extreme endurance events I have been able to help other people cure their ills and illnesses. Just like Jim Fixx said "Running is not a religion, Gatorade is not communion wine, and the Verrazano Bridge is not a Cathedral, and a sweaty warm up suit is not a surplice." Positive thinking can cure incurable diseases. The miracle of metaphysical healing (MH) contains dynamite to move mountains which are obstructing your health and your attainment of any desired goal. Through running and deep meditation I can attack and eliminate any kind of illness from areas of the body. This source of healing power is in us all: Within You! I have found the secret of MH, it is in the simple system for conditioning the mind to reject illness and embrace health. I use the Divine Creator's unlimited power of prayer to do miracles without becoming a religious freak. I believe the miracle power of my mind is the best medicine in any situation and the word "impossible" is not in my vocabulary. I have discovered through running, swimming and bicycling and other severe aerobic exercises we have a "higher self" full of wisdom, and also an "energized mind."

Now back to the race. I was sponsored by Cycle Peugeot (USA) and they covered the Nautilus Triathlon with a professional cameraman, Mr. Steve Lissou of Honolulu. He got some good pictures of my cheering section. I was so psyched up by the giant waves and roaring surf. There were some disappointing moments of the race for me. In the swim, I was caught in a big wave and washed ashore. Left high and dry thinking I was on a sand bar. I just clawed the sand with my hands and my powerful Furuhashi crawl, it is a six stroke crawl (a special sprinting stroke I learned by studying synchronizing swimming strokes). Even in slow motion it is difficult to analyze the Furuhashi crawl. So I checked out a book from the library on it but it was 64 pages of slow motion obscured by froth and bubbles. It became difficult to decode the strokes. My swimming teacher of the Rome family YMCA took an interest in me. She was amazed at my ability to process oxygen, and she surely thought I had oversized lungs.

I thought of my daughter's wedding again the morning of the triathlon. The cameras were flashing and clicking away, but the photographer missed three of the best shots of them all. The first shot was on the Kamehamemeha highway, down off the high mountains, near Sugar mill ruins at Kaswa Beach Park. I had my super Peugeot bike, going downhill at tremendous speed (estimated 35 miles per hour) when suddenly at the bottom of the hill a car stopped and began signaling for a left hand turn. I did not have time to pray, hitting the brakes, my feet were strapped in the "rat traps" (toe clips), the accident was over in a flash. I tried to pass on the right and was not too happy to test my new $45.00 Bell crash helmet in such a demanding way. The shoulder of the road had a 4 to 6 inch drop which when negotiated caused my bike to go out of control. The rough, bumpy surfaces made the bike (with me on it) airborne, jumping the guard rail and me and the bike landed in deep gravel filled ditch about 5 feet deep. Several injuries were sustained. The sharp gravel did a good job on my left knee. The impact of landing while still being stuck in the "rat traps" did my mind no good. The sharp gravel also did a good job on my groin, along with the two gear changing shifting levers which jabbed me so hard I thought it was a "double hernia." But, the main damage was done to my left hip which took the blunt of the fall. My left knee was bloody from one of the shifting levers which caught me in the groin. My left knee was a bloody mass of abrasions, scratches all over the knee area, my left knee was badly cut. The crash helmet had worked and it saved my life. A lady stopped her car and peered down at me asking if I were all right. I said, "Lady, I am the Senior Iron Man of the World, nothing can stop me." After digging the bike out of the ditch, I pulled the bike up the incline high embankment. The bike, unbelievably was not too badly damaged. Just a little misalignment, the brakes rubbed the wheel rim and caused me to expand more energy to ride the bike. Finally, I stretched the brake cable with my fingers with the force of the devil; it slackened and quit rubbing. The remaining ride took me to Haleiwa, Wahiawa, Waipahu, Peral City, Aiea, and past the airport and ended at Aloha Tower.

My second crash came on the Kamehameha Highway near Kahuku Sugar Mill where once again I became airborne when my bike ran off the shoulder of the road into a long water filled ditch. And I went into the ditch for the second time in less than half an hour. I was attached to the bike peddles by straps and the thin metallic toe clips used to give me toe lift when climbing mountains on my bike. This was an unusual accident; the bike flopped over the guard rail and I was lying on my back still seated and peddling the machine. Some fast action had to be accomplished to keep from drowning. The only thing which saved my life was my special quick release feature on the leather straps on the toe clips. By getting free from the bike, I was like "Houdini" and I turned over and crawled out of the water filled ditch. One good thing about this spill is that I did not get cut up as badly as the first accident, the best being a flash change into dry clothes.

Thankfully I did not fare too bad in the third accident. Leaving Haleiwae, past Waialua, on the route to Wahiawa, I came up against the Koolau mountains and rode my bike in granny gear for 6 miles, cranking away at about 30 miles per hour peddle speed, but not going anywhere fast. I was nearing the Appex and my brakes were partially on. Locked in the "rat traps," I made a strange discovery while riding high in the saddle, just stomping the peddles, it took much energy to overcome the pony brake action and climb the volcanic Koolau Mountains.

The 6 mile volcanic mountain trail did not stop me. I found myself pumping the bike peddles with all my might; however, what went wrong was unexpected. I stalled. I could not crank the peddles another turn. The 20 degree slope was too much. It came to a point where I could not move the peddles by standing up on them, the bike wobbled. It was too late to react. I tumbled off the road bank into a volcanic crater, bump, bump, bump. I tumbled down the jagged rocks, lodging in clumps of grass and weeds. I lay there in shock. My crew just sat in the Toyota truck and their hair turned gray. After a few minutes, my hand reached over the road bank and tugged at a clump of grass, then my white helmet surfaced then my arm came into view with the bike. My crew was happy to see me alive. My bike was still rideable but out of alignment, the backup bike was shot, I had wrecked the derailer on it. Steve the photographer did not get a picture of this accident because he had taken Karen, back to Honolulu and was waiting at the finish line of the bike ride at Alhoa tower for me to show up.

Warren McCullen, who had run the Pheidippides marathon with me was just like a father. He shouted, gave me explicit instructions and sounded like a real commander in chief. I was in a weakened state and needed to be dealt with sternly. My blood sugar was low and my reflexes were becoming slower.

Close encounters were everywhere. Each passing vehicle was a threat to my safety. Warren and Bob watched closely. It was dark about 9:00 p.m. Bob in several occasions had to pick me up and literally sit me on the bike, then put my feet into the "rat traps," pull the leather straps and give me a giagantic catapultic action "G" thrust and yell "Go For It, Huck."

The bike ride finished at Aloha Tower and one of the race officials gave me a massage on my legs using some analgesic balm that got the circulation going again. I jogged in place a few minutes, could not get forward propulsion from the cranking action of the bike ride, but slowly they started to move ahead.

I waited for a while so Steve Lissau, the photographer could get some good shots of me. The china Clipper ship was docked alongside a peer, and I posed again for the photographer. After running about a mile, Carol buzzed by in her yellow, shiny Jaguar and threw a few kisses my way. This really perked me up so I started chasing the Jag, faster and faster. My goutish toe was sending out SOS's by the central nervous system hot line but I started turing on my magnetic generator and in about 10 miles of running all the pain had left my toe.

Then I "Hit The Wall." The sprint with the Jag and Carol did me in. Every ounce of strength suddenly dwindled. Carol disappeared in her Jag, I never saw her again, but will always remember her smile.

I was like "mush." There was no glycogen left in my hamstrings and quads, I had low blood sugar, like death I staggered into a ditch. Crawling out, I hobbled and walked for about 100 yards. I spotted my crew with the Toyota. I asked them for a cup of coffee to keep me awake, but they didn't have any. Then I remembered the bottle of caffeine tablets that was used instead of coffee which released the fatty acids into my blood stream. I tossed in a caffeine tablet, chewed it up and then chased it with a glass of orange juice. In 3 minutes I was suddenly awake and from some unknown source, somehow synthesized the fatty acids in my blood, I had taken a catalyst and was now burning protein: I did not have a lot of fat on my body, my total body fat weight was about 3%, but all I knew was that my feet were flying and my crew began to wonder what had happened to Huck. I sprinted the last 13 miles from Haeaii Kai back to the finish line. I really showed them at the finish line how a Senior Citizen can kick.

After I crossed the finish line at 2:18:35 am. on 1/13/80, I grabbed a beer; the crew tried to find a "bottle of champagne" but the liquor stores were closed at 11:00 p.m. I was taken back to the Coral Sea Motel, for a hot shower and did not wake up until 9:00 a.m. I held a press conference at 10:00 a.m., the awards ceremony was held in the afternoon.

I shook hands with the race director and remembered back 7 years prior when the electrocardiograph operator told me to see my lawyer and make out my will and if I was still alive to go and see my doctor. I smiled, having turned old age back again for at least another 10 years.

I received a lot of publicity for both Peugeot and myself. The papers carried nice articles on me and a post newspaper feature was prepared by the Honolulu Advertiser.

Warren and Kathy took me to the airport.

We met Diana Nyad, the World Champion Swimming Ace, she swam from Cuba to Florida twice. Only one time she had to abort the swim, she was attacked my a Portugese Man of War. She carries a scar across her throat.

CHAPTER 11

BOSTON MARATHON (4 TIMES)

When I think back to the 83rd Boston Marathon in April 1979, the thing most remembered was the weather. It was damp and chilly with a slight drizzle that added to the bone chilling dampness. There were literally thousands of runners hovering in the Hopkinton Gym, avoiding the harsh elements. At that moment I had no idea of the impending gloom that would shatter my world in the few short weeks to follow.

The field that day appeared to be over 7,000 runners. Therefore my starting position was about a quarter of a mile back of the start line, down a slight hill. I fell into the 3:30 grouping near the rear of the line in front of the slight hill that the non official runners called "bandits," where I had lined up for the two previous years when I had been a bandit myself. I failed to meet the qualifying time standard of 3:30 for a previous marathon within the year preceding the Boston Marathon.

With the slow start and taking five minutes to get to the starting line, I had a lot of time to make up which meant I would have to go a sub-eight pace average. My watch read 44 minutes at the five mile mark and I had closed the gap even further at ten mile with a reading of 81 for the split. I still had a chance at 20 with a 2:39, but the fast pace and the expenditure of energy getting up Heartbreak Hill had left me in good condition for the undertaker.

The crowd kept urging me on and they called me by the name of my T-shirt, "Incredible Huck" and one fellow asked me if those vitamins (Thompson's) my sponsor had written on my T-shirt did me any good? I told him that I was 80 years old and chasing my 85 year old pregnant wife who was a mile ahead of me. He laughed and said he would try some himself.

I should have popped a dozen more that morning because I had run out of the money by five minutes, it would have made no difference because the Boston Athletic Association (BAA), in charge of the Boston Marathon, a few days later changed the standards to 3:10 for the master runners, including 50-60 and over age brackets. This was a 20 minute handicap which meant almost a minute a mile faster pace, that for me, not being a speed merchant, was with my available training schedule the same as asking Bill Rodgers to run a sub two hour marathon. In truth he would have more of a chance running 2:00 than me a 3:10.

Looking down at the number X713 pinned on my T-shirt that day had a great significance to me and at that point it seemed that the Boston Marathon had become my only reason to live. It was the culmination of seven years of the hardest training I had ever done for just over 3 hours and half of the hardest work, for a lot of memories to last me the rest of my life.

I remember Betty Forte, who lives in Wellsley with her husband Mike, chief engineer for a major electronics corporation in Boston, running out to meet me with a large pitcher of orange juice downtown in Wellsley. Yes, running Boston is mentally refreshing and rewarding. The frustration is searching for the words to describe it.

It was a month later at Athens, Greece that I decided to picket the BAA for changing their standards. I fed the results available into my minicomputer and it indicated a great deal of discrimination in the way they were going to set up their new standards. Forty four percent of the younger (open age division) runners were disqualified. 41% of the girls were disqualified but 65% of the masters were disqualified out of the 6,000 plus runners completing the 1979 Boston Marathon.

During my running the Phedippides Marathon 3 times nonstop, I had envisioned running Boston 4 times nonstop. To accomplish this meant a lot of long distance running and ultra marathoning. I chose races like the Western States 100 mile Ultimate challenge over the High Sierra Nevada Mountains in California, the Lake Waramaug 50 miler. I ran the Mayors Jewelers 100 KM (62 miles) Ultra in Miami, Florida. I trekked over the Appalachian mountains in the JFK 50 mile run, the Trail to Infinity, and completed the Hawaiian Triathton, the premier endurance event of the world; swimming 2.4 miles in open seas, biking 112 miles over the Koolau mountains, circumnavigating the Isle of Oahu; then running a 26.2 miler back to back over the hilly Hawaiian marathon course, for a total of 140.6 miles. There were other ultra marathons during that year, like the 50 mile Frankfort to Louisville, Ky. Then Allentown, Pa. Shaeffer 50 miler and 20 marathons plus some mountain run up Whiteface mountain about one mile high, and Equinox mountain, about 4,000 feet in elevation.

In all my 1979 marathons I never came close to a 3:10. I flirted with death time and time again, running just on the edge of succumbing, still not improving enough, I needed more than a breakthrough, nothing short of a leg transplant would do me any good. All year I had run marathons, on the edge of death only a little fine filament remained attaching my life to my body; it was just like a frayed rope holding by a single thread. It reminded me of flying myself like a kite where I would rise up to the clouds and hang onto that struggling self, running on the road below, like a puppet, held by a small string; the chemical balance of life and the interwoven mysteries of spirit and soul. I would lash time and time again my body with my mind, and beat my body with a bloody chain within my subconscious. At times I would literally climb out of my body, sit on my shoulders and just like a jockey boot myself and use the mental quirt to force every gram of energy and speed from a fleshy skeleton that exceeded the limitations by such a wide margin that stress fractures, torn ligaments, and ripped sinews made it appear that crippling MS had taken over, time and again Boston eluded me.

Two weeks prior to the 1980 Boston Marathon, I published my press release and it hit the radio, newspapers, and the news wire service. At this time I wished to make as many waves as possible to let the millions of fellow runners, who also felt they had been discriminated against, know I had taken things into my own feet and was going to protest the unfair qualifying standards. My own immediate running group, the Roman runners, and friends from all over the nation, and many foreign countries supported me and had faith in my doing the run. My biggest problem was with the Boston press. They seemed determined to force me into a low profile. They instead only hurt Boston, the air lines, transportation carriers, restaurants hotels and motels. It was easy to get a room in all the normally filled places. Some estimates showed the City of Boston and surrounding areas suffered an estimated loss of over $5,000,000 in 1980 because of the small turnout due to the unfair standards imposed by the BAA.

On Friday night, April 18, the final preparation for the Epic Protest run was completed. My crew consisted of Tom Wilson and John McGee. Tom, McGee and I quickly left for a press interview with the local newspaper. Utica Observer dispatch. Their reporter Howard Groff met us at their Rome office local headquarters and Howard prepared his feature story, took photographs and left us his phone number to call when the protest run was completed. He expected it would get more attention; however, the press was too busy with Rosie Ruiz to care even about the real winners. The 1980 Boston Marathon was sabotaged by Rosie, it was her race, she had become a household word, now and forever in the running world.

Saturday morning at 6:00 a.m. Tom, McGee and I left in his new Chevy pickup, its cab loaded with support gear for Boston. The logistics for the epic run were phenomenal. The planning and organization reminded me of a huge amphibious assault, force landing on some unknown beached head. The contingencies were enormous. What would the weather be like? Would there be sunshine, rain, cold, hot weather, high winds or calm, or a combination of all. The clothing selection for the run would in itself be a major consideration. Would I need a windbreaker, rain suit, thermal underwear, nylon shorts, wool socks, cotton socks, wool cap, cotton cap, or rain hat, head and sweatband sock cap or visor? It was decided that six pair of running shoes would be a wise choice, two pair of water proofed in case of rain, and two pair a couple of sizes larger in case my feet swelled or developed injury. I carried along my Osagas with the new tread in case a snowfall might plague me. I threw in half dozen pair of running socks, wool and cotton, a half dozen T-shirts, sweaters and underwear. Other support items included portable cb radios for communication between the support truck and bicycle, flashlight, some batteries, disposable flashlights, two bicycles, tool kit, extra inner tubes, patches, a pump, bottles of water, orange juice, liquid fructose, Shaklee energy bars, oranges, apples, bananas, gator aid, ERG (gookinaid), Ergogenic aids consisting of 31 bottles of Shaklee and Thompson and other manufacturers vitamin/minerals, caffeine, jackets, warm up suits, movie camera, press type camera, extra file, ace crepe bandages, hand aids, ice bucket, drinking cups, aspirin, DMSO, spray anti septic, banaleg (analgesic), cramer skin lube (very heavy cream petroleum jelly), plus my reflective shoulder band and jacket to run during the night on the highway. In addition to these and numerous other items. I had to pack all the presentation material for the press conference, there were flip charts showing a computerized shred out of the 1979 finishers, indicating the percentages of unfairness to all age group catagories caused by the new standards. I had several letters which I received from sympathetic runners with me and expressing their dislike for the way the Boston Marathon was being run. In the huge presentation package I had photographs of me running the Pheidippides Marathon in Athens three times (78 miles), and pictures of my crossing the High Sierra Nevada Mountains for 100 miles in California. I had pictures of myself on the track doing the Miami 100 KM run, and Hawaiian triathlon.

The purpose of these photographs and credentials were to prove to the press and the BAA that I had the experience and ability to run for over a hundred miles and it was not a hoax, but a sincere protest in which I represented thousands of runners in the nation and throughout the world.

Tom drove us to Boston in his new truck, we turned off the Massachusetts turnpike at the Hopkinton exit and we followed the Boston Marathon route to Boston while McGee made notes and plotted the course on a map and made notes of significant landmarks. We arrived at the Colonnade Hotel where I arranged for reservations for a press conference room. I also ordered some choice wine for the press and any BAA official that might show up because of their interest in the protest run; in the 30,000,000 joggers, runners, racers that were interested in the Boston Marathon.

We arranged the presentation material in our conference room and waited from 2:00 to 4:00 p.m. for any news media or officials to show up. I had sent them telegrams three days earlier and a news release ten days prior explaining my intent to demonstrate against the unfair standards, and inviting them to the conference.

At 6:00 pm. Tom, McGee and I left for the Elliott hotel for spaghetti. We returned to the hotel at 8:00 p.m. at which time I called the radio TV, and newspapers informing them of a change in time schedule. We had decided, in view of the impending heat wave that by starting at 5:45 a.m., I would have two more hours of daylight to run in and arrive at Hopkinton before the noon day heat struck. This was a good and bad change, as will be shown later. One radio station announcer I talked with told me he just could not believe that any human could cover the course four times and his friends felt the same. "Those hills will destroy any man," he said. This remark only psyched me up the more and I sat on the edge of the bed gritting me teeth and clenching my fists. I had run over 100 miles before but they were over some of the damndest mountains in the USA. I was forgetting the most important thing to run it in reverse from the Pru to Hopkinton, there is about 600 feet elevation gain and includes running up Heartbreak Hill from the opposite direction, all this reduces the legs to rubber.

At 4:30 am. after spending a restless night I awoke and gazed out the 9 story window at the panoramic maze of lights, the big prudential building, the Sheraton, the Christian Science building. I felt like a spaceman about to be fired into orbit; all my systems were on "Go." I gulped down 31 vitamins and ate a Shaklee energy bar. We checked out of the hotel and walked over to the marathon finish line in front of the big Pru. Tom and McGee took movie pictures and photographs of me about to start the epic run. A lone delivery truck passed by and a policewoman in a prowl car just sat there paying little attention to us. We agreed to meet on commonwealth Ave at 5:40 a.m. sharp. I toed off the finish line to start the 104.8 mile jaunt, while the crew headed for the truck while I ran towards Herford Street.

The temperature was about 50 degrees and I wore my red show off jacket, the one with dozens of marathon patches on it, immodestly displaying "The Incredible Huck" on the back in 3 inch letters, I felt really frisky. My stride was fluid and graceful with spring in my feet; the press was still sound asleep awaiting the Rosie story which would occur later the next day. The thing I worried about the most never happened. The police did not lock me up for picketing the Boston Marathon. My T-shirt read, "The Boston Marathon is Unfair to runners" in large block letters and the word "unfair" was printed in red letters. The same was true of my support crew; I had T-shirts like mine made for them.

My crew arrived to meet me at Commonwealth Avenue; they were waiting for me near Bill Rodger's sport store just around the corner. After reaching Heartbreak Hill, McGee started his bicycle support. From his bike he gave me cups of orange juice and water. I had shed the warm up jacket now, but soon the divided highway ran out. I had to jump up and down the curbs, not being able to run in the street, during the heavy traffic. The jumping up and down the curbs put an extra strain on my hamstrings and flexors. The steady elevation gain kept "zapping" my legs. I clearly remember running past a road sign which read Newton. At Newton I spotted another police car, but he just kept on going and did not seem to care if I was picketing the Boston Marathon, now some 30 hours before the race would start.

At close to 8:00 am. running past Wellesley, a young girl met me running. She asked me why the statement on the T-shirt, I yelled back at her and said the BAA took 10 minutes off the girls time qualifying standards for the marathon and I was protesting for them by running the course four times nonstop. "All Right," she said and keep on running. I continued to pass lots of other girls there and help out my hand for them, and delivered my message to them. They were all pleased to hear someone was protesting for them. The heat started to build up by 10:00 am., it was up to 75 degrees and rising rapidly. At that time I had already completed running to Hopkinton. I took me 4:10 to do the first 26.2 miles, running uphill from the Pru. Many of my friends and fellows that I had run ultra marathons with cheered me along the way. A fellow from Boston that had been in the Hawaiian triathton with me in January met me at Hopkinton. I assumed the press were in seclusion with the BAA, they did not even send out a photographer.

The return marathon was more eventful than the initial run. The temperature continued to rise by 2:00 p.m., the mercury reached 88 degrees in the areas close to Heartbreak Hill. The truck van was on my side of the road which helped, running the first marathon I had to cross from time to time for aid, I must have did an extra mile crossing the road. McGee continued to help me by riding alongside with his bike, trying to get some smoothness in my running style which was becoming rapidly sloppy. Visions of anger turned unremorsefully painful. My legs cramped from loss of electrolytes and my gait turned into a "stiff legged shuffle." I met a doctor who was near my age running up Heartbreak Hill, he was going to run unofficially and chatted with me for a long time. In fact he ran all the way to near Bill Roger's sports shop on commonwealth Avenue. At the fire house in Newton, at the foot of the hills where you turn the corner, my friend caught me walking, trying to get the cramps out of my legs. I thought it was someone from the press, as he had a professional camera. I put on a wind sprint for him and tripped up and stumbled for about 15 feet, but kept on jogging up Heartbreak Hill. I tried a cup of coffee to get caffeine into my blood stream to release the fatty acids, hopeful that it would help me synthesize my fat and protein faster. It worked. I picked up the pace at 4:00p.m. and arrived back at the Big Pru, 52.4 miles behind me.

Tom and McGee were there to take pictures and shoot some film of me crossing the finish line. Another runner told me to wait a few minutes while he ran across the street to a store and bought me a coca cola. I jogged in place, waiting for the coke. Many runners asked me questions about the run and joined in with their own gripes that the press did not cover the feature story.

At about 4:30 p.m., I was headed up Herford Street and on the way to rendezvous with my crew waiting close to Bill Roger's sports store about 3 miles away. My legs were getting better and by alternating running and walking, I made it to the top of Heartbreak Hill. The sun was setting and darkness started to close in quickly. The truck van was on the opposite side of the road so I had to cross the road many times to get aid. McGee still rode his bike. I had hoped he could have used my famous triathlon white Peugeot bike that someone had stolen from my cellar two days before we left my home, and later returned.

At Newton it was dark. I put on my reflective shoulder band and continued onward. At Wellesley my stride became cramped, the cool night air made the muscles very stiff. By then my steps were about 6 inches and getting shorter. At this point I started popping caffeine tablets and rubbing my legs with Banalog, an analgesic so strong it would limber up a petrified hamstring.

The headlights from the cars were blinding and McGee rode and walked along side his bike holding a flashlight. I thought about the words Will Cloney had said, "he hoped I did not get lost or run over by a car." Getting lost was not the problem; there was not inches between me and the automobiles, especially when I ran next to the guard rail alongside the lake. It was really risky and slowed me down even further. By this time I drank liquid fructose and took my potassium tablets to get some strength back into my leg muscles. The uphill course was terrible and demanding. I was doubling up on my dolomite and eating Shaklee energy bars about every two hours, and taking zinc tablets to heal up the tissue teardown. Even with all the fructose intake my blood sugar continued to decline and I could feel hypoglycemia coming on. Now, the night air added to the energy demise and hypothermia set in. This was controlled by a dry T-shirt and a wind breaker.

It was midnight before I arrived back at Hopkinton. The strangest sight up till then we had seen, at the start line, was a runner in his warm-ups just standing there waiting. I told him I had just run 78.6 miles and he said he was going to camp out on the start line so he could get an early start at noon tomorrow. I think he drove from Michigan for the race. It was all downhill now except for the jaunt up Heartbreak Hill for the fourth consecutive time. I crammed an energy bar, banana and some fructose tablets in my pocket along with a caffeine tablet and took off to get the farce over with. I ran on the left side of the road going back, it was safer and the oncoming cars were visible.

Fatigue had set in and my mind started playing tricks on me. I could imagine all kinds of weird things but kept on jogging and walking. Then, it happened; my stiff legged shuffle became a "death run." At Wellesley my stomach started cramping up and I had to walk slowly, sort of hunched over by holding my hand against my stomach I could stand the pain. By then I had gone into a hypnotic trance and was running and walking on sheer guts alone. All the glycogen had long ago disappeared. I was chomping on the "ultra bullet" and had gone into an oxygen debt so many times I had become bankrupt hours ago. The needle in my mental tachometer was in the red scale, now I just wanted to go the distance. I felt like I had infantile paralysis in both hamstrings and calf muscles. The frisky lunacy which I had started 20 hours ago had become subservient to the sanity of pain and agony; it was now "Survival." It reminded me of a New York to Nome, Alaska fun run. I would not even get a T-shirt or a free meal when it was over. Now, I ran with a bizarre kind of obsession, through the chill and darkness. "This is horrible," I thought. At that point I never wanted to hear the word "Run" or any of that verb's conjugations again. I just tried to disassociate my mind from the pain in my body, my mind was getting foggy. I had used a lot of brain cells for fuel after glycogen and fat reserves were depleted. Brain cells are protein and they burn up quickly in emergency conditions. I went into self hypnosis, mediation, mantas, prayers, and called all the saints in heaven by name; using my pipeline to the Creator of the Universe, but the only message that came back was, "if it is to be, it's up to me."

The run from Wellesley to Heartbreak Hill was a blur. I kept on going in and out of consciousness. I dimly remember next running down Commonwealth Avenue around Bill Roger's sports store and kept on. The sunshine was warm on my face. Some fellow ran into a café near Elliott's lounge and bought me a cup of coffee. I guzzled it down and continue towards the finish line. Looking down at my J.C. Penny Olympic brand shoes, they were filthy dirty, soot and dust was all over me. My socks were a sad sight. Sweat had caked with grime and some bloody lymph was oozing from my left shoe near the middle toe. The gobs of skin lube had soaked through the nylon fabric.

I turned into Herford Street and it was an uphill grade for one block. The sunshine felt wonderful on my face, the hypothermia from the chilly night air left goose bumps on my legs. While jogging up Herford Street, my mind drifted and I started running backwards instead of forwards, it was total disorientation!

The sun was bringing me to; it was like a slap in the face. For the last 3 miles, had the most violent stomach cramps. It felt like my pancreas had collapsed from pumping insulin to overcome the coca cola which I had drunk, knowing full well it was the worst thing to take at that time. For a time I thought the oyster shells, eggshells and dolomite from the Cal Mag tablets had gotten into my appendix. My form was terrible, sort of doubled over. Tears were dripping off the end of my nose. There it was, at last, Boylson Street. I tried to kick but could only jog to the finish line. The last thing I remember was a big Irish policeman by the name of Mike Craven at the finish line who helped me keep my balance and asked what it was all about.

My body was stippled with pain and agony, but I forced a smile for Mike and told him about the run. He said he ran some up until a year ago, but now he was going right out and start again. My Epic Protest was over. Now, over 30,000,000 spurned joggers, runners, and racers could know Huckaby carried the picket sign for them, just like the sign on the truck read, "The 20th of April 1980 was the day when Huck socked it to the BAA."

I crossed the finish line at 6:10:15. That was 24 hours, 30 minutes and 15 seconds after I had begun. I looked like death warmed over. One fella pulled me over and said, "Are you gonna run the Boston Marathon?" "You don't look like you are going to make it to your hotel room."

I went over to the Sheraton Hotel and called the Globe. They said, "Wait in the lobby and a reporter would take my picture and get my story." I went into the lobby and hung around a few minutes, then the floor bouncer came over and said I looked so scroungy, would I mind sitting on a bench back behind a partition. I waited for about half an hour, but the press never showed up. Then a lovely lady by the name of Paula Winn, waiting for her friend Jerry Pooler from Dallas Texas asked me for my story. She was joyful and elated. She said Jerry was in charge of the movement to get more time for the masters and he would join forces with me. We exchanged letters as time passed and his write up in the runner's world a while back about the Dallas, Texas run showed him to be really spaced out on the running and to get a shot at officially running Boston would make the doctor happy.

The press never showed. I called the radio stations but they said they had a big story about the new woman winner of the Boston Marathon, Rosie Ruiz!

Note: Rosie Ruiz was crowned but disqualified when they found out she jumped in the race and ran around the block!

CHAPTER 12

MEMPHIS RUNNING MADNESS

Halloween night, with its entire bewitching heritage, was only moments away. All over the nation children were primed up for their yearly trick or treating antics.

The plane on which I had booked passage carried several other ultra-marathoners and myself from New York, banked sharply and descended to the Memphis International airport. A brilliant sunset was visible through the porthole windows of the plane and below to the Mississippi river 10,000 feet below. Now three states were visible across the serpentine river, West Memphis, Arkansas and a mile to the south sprawled the city of Southaven, Mississippi, and on the horizon loomed the city of Memphis with its skyscrapers silhouetted against the sunset.

Memphis, the legendary city, home of Elvis Presley appeared to be the running capital of the mid-south. Several parks were clearly visible. Auburn Park, T.O. Fuller State Park and Oberton Park where the Memphis Art Academy is located. Runners could be seen doing their training. At Oberton park the Third Goblin Gallop running extravaganza was scheduled to start at midnight with a 2.5 mile costume fun run, followed by a 12 hour ultra-marathon around a 2.5 mile loop around the park, then a series of 10km events at 2 PM., followed by a 24 hour run on the field track at Memphis State University. These races would start at 4:00 p.m. Saturday until 4:30 Sunday afternoon.

Gerry Vannoy (37), was the race director of the Memphis full Moon Runners' Club. These races were the spearhead of the modern day "fun runs." Gerry had changed the banal and often boring feeling of entering "just another race" by capitalizing on the special holidays to bring the sneaker footed runners out of the woodwork with these unique races, including races on Valentine's Day, Leap year (Sadie Hawkins Day), Thanksgiving, Halloween and other colorful holidays. He pioneered a new running movement, gaining friends and followers all over the nation. Gerry had become race director quite by accident. He purchased a number of T-shirts for a race and when it was over he had a huge surplus on hand. This meant he had to hold another race to get rid of the T-shirts. Alas, over 300 runners showed up! He had to go out and buy more. "It's been like this ever since," Vannoy said. Now his attic looks like a warehouse, loaded with T-shirts, trophies and other parpanalia used at races: like flags, marker poles, water canisters packages and cartons of ERG, Gatoraid, Body punch, Break-time, chains for finishing chutes, card tables for aid station drinks: and his garage is loaded with race support items also. Gerry's wife, Becky, is an enthusiastic runner. Becky outran Gerry in the Sadie Hawkins Day race, and Gerry ended up before marrying Sam!

Gerry became a full fledged race director because of his enthusiasm and devotion to the sport of running. His Cupid's Chase on Valentine's Day, and his T-shirts with a pink cupid with bow and arrow were a smashing success with runners. But his greatest extravaganza was the race which I entered. "The Goblin Gallop."

Three years ago he held the first Halloween "fun run" Goblin Gallop, a 2 1/2 mile run around the perimeter of Overton park in Memphis. This race became the most talked about race in the south. Runners travel from all over the nation just to enter the weekend of running events. Gerry, personally, met the ultra-marathon runners who arrived by air and transported them to the Big apple restaurant for last minute carbos and then to the runners clinic.

At the runners clinic three ultra-marathoners and myself were requested to speak and give out highly informative data on running. James Robertson (18) from Prospect park; Kevin Donahue (28) from the Melrose track club in New York City. Richard Hackney (26) from Dallas Texas and myself from Rome, New York, one of the world's most prolific ultra-marathoners helped to keep the auditorium in a state of exuberance and awe. We gave out ultra-marathoning information from convential books and magazines, covered subjects like ultra stretching, aerobic dancing, the diet of diets, loading made easy, pace, energy conservation, ultra running style, ergogenic aids, special equipment, training schedules and discussed my special liniment which would revitalize a petrified hamstring. We had a very informative Q&A session. We discussed how to avoid injury. Steroids were unknown back then.

My topic was metaphysical healing, positive thinking, how to send an aura to control the atoms of the body, self hypnosis meditation, mantas, prayers. As a born again runner the Almighty revitalized my body and to Him I give credit for running races which stagger the mind.

At 11:00 p.m., Richard Hackney and I started making preparations for the most unthinkable running parley; we had entered every running event to be held over the weekend. We didn't have a motel room, there was no need of one, our plans were to throw our suitcases under a tree and run the 2 ½ mile loop for the next 12 hours until we could get over to the Memphis State track and run around our suitcases again for another 24 hours, after which I would catch my plane for Rome, New York and Ritchie would hop on his motor cycle and drive 500 miles back to Dallas.

The first event was a 2 ½ mile costume run at 11:00 p.m. Dozens of runners in costumes were beginning to pour into the art academy and stood in line to register or pick up their pre registered packets. There were an odd variety of unusual garbs—the Cat Girl in sneakers, Spiderman with a rope around his neck, strange spooks, haunts, Batman and assorted Frankensteins in Adidas, Brooks, New Balance, Etonics, Pumas, Pro Keds, Tigers, Osagas, JCPenny's Oyympics, Convairs, Pony's and many other national brand running shoes.

In the art academy runners were gathering in large numbers. The atmosphere became electrified with noisy chatter, goblins were lining up at the front of the academy, getting ready for the start of midnight; it was one big gathering of trick or treaters carrying flashlights, jack-o-lanterns, and some were barefoot. A dog clad in a full moon runners T-shirt wagged its tail in joyful salutation.

There were special prizes for the various categories, including best male and female, speeders, fastest accountant, lawyer, doctor, dentist, city official, news reporter, preacher, policeman, sorority girl, trucker, bare foot runner, democrat, republican, outpatient (must have had 1980 operation with more than six stitches), fastest unknown comic; plus many others.

At about 5 minutes before the race, Richard Hackney put on his Groucho Marx mustache and I threw a bed sheet over my head with huge fluorescent yellow letters "Hoblin Goblin" printed on the back. The instructions were when the horn blew, the race was on. Suddenly came the blast which set over 300 howling goblins into orbit into the thick of competition.

The female dog clad in the full moon runners T-shirt won first prize as the best dressed runner. The fastest barefooted runners had to show the bottoms of their feet to prove they had run the course and really hoofed it sans chaussuers de coureur. Ritchie and I galloped along and finished in about 26 minutes. I won for the fastest in the unknown comic category, receiving both a plaque and T-shirt.

The race went through the park and down spooky streets, amidst howling screeching, soul harrowing, and nerve shattering sounds. It was sensational and worth every bit of effort expanded. I checked my watch to establish a pace I could hold for the next 12 hours and ran at a 10 minute mile pace to conserve energy as I had covered the course many times (in fact I did cover it 20 1/2 times more in the 12 hour run (for a total of 51 miles). The midnight 2.5er was won by Don Diekes.

After the race was completed and the trophies given out, the costumed runners had an all night party in the park, eating lunches, drinking and chattering but a heavy dew set in and they left by about 2:30 a.m., the temperature dropped to the mid forties.

Richie and I toed the line having thrown sanity to the goblins and at 1:00 am., at the command of "Go" from Gerry Vannoy, we started our 12 hour "fun run" in conjunction with a couple dozen hardy and crazy harriers—it was very simple, all that was required was to start at 1:00 a.m. and keep it up until 1:00 p.m. The awards went to the 25 runners with the most miles. Tom Ulk (Milwaukee) won it with 75 miles; Ron Homan (Cookeville, Tenn) with 70 miles took second; Mike Sandrin (Arkansas with 65 miles took third and tied with Adam Lenning (Kentucky). I took it easy, saving something for my 24 hour run and 10KM race to follow and took 8th place with 51 miles.

A welcomed delay, I had to give first aid to my running friend Richie. Richie worked for a Dallas moving company and drove a truck for them. He loaded tons of furniture into his big truck and drove it daily. How did he run his training runs? Well, he ran 10 to 20 miles while leaving his bulldog in the cab to guard it while he ran in the wee hours of the morning, along the highway and by ways.

Richie rode his big Yamaha motorcycle up from Dallas, over 500 miles to run the weekend. I also was a native of Texas, my great grandfather had moved there from near Memphis back in 1850. I was born in a little cow town of Ranger, Texas over 60 years ago, and as a young boy I chased road runners, sage hens, and coyotes. At the age of 5 my father told me about Phidippides and I would spend hours running after jack rabbits. Little did I realize 55 years later I would be running enough miles monthly to take me across the state of Texas.

Richie and I had covered about 12 miles when suddenly Richie let out a scream and doubled over in pain. He had tripped over a pot hole and presumably ruptured himself. While Richie groaned in agonizing pain, I designed and fashioned a truss from an ace bandage and an athletic supporter, some adhesive tape, with the intention of getting him out of the race, at the end of the lap, and taking an ambulance to the nearest hospital. Richie proved himself to be the toughest of the though. He ran over 52 miles more with the hernia. Upon returning home to Dallas, his doctor examined him and found the incision had healed. An operation was not required. All that remained was a slight symptom, like a groin pull. Richie took to the road within a week, after the unfortunate accident. The doctor said, "Thanks to Huck he had avoided serious injury."

A Marine Sergeant, Mike Nordstrand, from the marine base near Memphis ran almost the equivalent of nearly 2 marathons; over 50 miles and he had never attempted a marathon before. He was amazed to find he had finished in 9th place and had lots of steam left. I paced Mike and explained early in the run "how to disconnect the brain from the body" and after a rest Richie joined us and we all ran through the night until the sky turned pink and the sun appeared on the horizon.

Some of the things of interest became apparent in the daylight, like the increased elevation the beautiful shrubbery, statues, tree lined roads and drinking fountains. After running since midnight by flashlight, it was a welcome sunrise. We had completed our 20th 2.5 mile lap and with only 15 minutes left, the race director put us on a one mile loop to finish out the 12 hour run.

Upon completion of the 12 hour "fun run," Richie and I had a few minutes to prepare for the 10KM serious run. We chug-a-lugged a half pint of liquid fructose, ate a few bananas, and I downed my 31 vitamins.

After a brief ceremony, while the trophies were being given out for the 12 hour run, several hundred fresh, eager runners were signing up for the 10 KM run. I had just completed 53.5 miles now to go ahead with these speed merchants. I said to myself, "its stress fracture roulette." At 2:00 p.m. the whistle blew, off the runners went. Richie got caught up in the "prop wash" of their sneakers and was burning the course when at the 2 mile mark he came to his senses and slowed to an 8 minute pace and continued to hold it with me to finish in a respectable 51 minutes which was not too swift but by that time with the hernia action he was not searching for excuses-he did not need to prove a thing.

We picked up our third T-shirt of the weekend and quickly Gerry shuttled us in his van over to the Memphis state university field track for the 24 hour run. Top runners were already setting up their tables at the track, including Dave Obelkevich of the Melrose track club and James Robertson of prospect park ultra team: both from New York city. Also from New York city was Kevin Donahue, Jim Jones (Memphis), Don Morgan of Memphis, Don Bassard of Ft. Wayne, Indiana, Herb Moriarty (Memphis), Pati Baylock (Memphis), and Crystal Wilkerson (Memphis).

The 24 hour run got underway at 4:30 p.m. with Dave Obelkevich attempting to set a new record for the 50 miler and 100 KM along the way. Dave ran like a machine; he had trained hard for this one. At Flushing Meadows on lucky Friday the 13th, Dave covered the 100 miles in 14:51:12, which means he averaged a 8:54 pace. On 9/30/79 on his 36th birthday he covered the famous London to Brighton course in 6:24:47 (a 7:05 pace) and in December 1979 he ran 100 KM (62.2 miles) in 7:07:35 (only 10 other American runners have broken 8 hours for this distance). In May 1970 at forest Park, NY City 40 miler, he twisted his ankle at 23 miles, put on an ace bandage and finished in 11th place out of 70 good runners. Dave had run his first marathon in 1974 in 4:20:00 on just 6 miles per week training. He proves that runners don't have to run 100 miles per week, which many runners have become so accustomed to believe. His current training schedule is a low 70 to 80 miles per week. Dave ran 15 marathons and 13 ultra-marathons since December 1979.

The chill of the night air caused the runners to cramp up. I gave them some of my horse liniment which freed their muscles. Keeping on Dave's heels was the youngest ultra-marathoner, James Robertson (18) from New York City prospect park ultra team. Jimmy is a junior at the academy of Aeronautics in Queens. He was born in British Guinna and started running at the age of 7. He's been running faster and longer for the past 11 years. Jimmy excelled in high and broad jumping and his legs are more flexible than a kangaroo. He trained under some good ultra-marathoners, including the famous Cahit Yeter and Paul Soskind acting like coaches. He also does aerobic dancing to keep his legs in shape for the ultras. Normally, ultra-marathoners do not develop before an age of 30, which means that Jimmy will be a threat of the future if he continues to progress and may have a shot at the records. He ran the New York City marathon, under 3 hours at the age of 15, and used this year's New York City marathon as a depletion run. He covered the distance in a swift 2:50, tops in his age group.

The 24 hour ultra-marathon proved to be a well managed affair, although Gerry Vannoy did not have a computer, nevertheless the timing was accurate and precise. The race officials manually recorded each lap of every runner and gave splits as records were involved; the track had been certified and approved.

Becky worked into the wee hours of the morning during which was referred to the "longest night." The heavy dew fell on everything, including the recording girl's hair. Becky said it was eerie and weird how the dew fell upon their hair and trickled down their faces. It was cool and damp, in the mid 40's during the early morning hours, and the runners began to cramp up but they managed to keep going by using some special analgesic Huck supplied. The most warming substance that was served was hot broth which helped fight the cold. The university dorms were located alongside the track only about 10 feet off the edge of the track. They let the runners use the rest rooms, however, someone locked them at midnight and the world became their garbage cans, as runners fled into the nearby shrubbery.

The sharp chill caused Dave Obelkevich to slow and he realized that he was not going to break the 50 mile or 100 KM record as cramps plagued him in the pre midnight time frame, and slowed second place Jimmy Robertson and third place runner up Kevin Donahue. For a while Richie had to "bite the ultra bullet" and catch a wink as the pain in his groin was unbearable. I just kept running and jogging around the track and occasionally hoofed it for a lap to stretch my hamstrings. I was trying to set a PR for myself and try to cover as many miles in the 24 hours as I could, which included my previous runs. I wanted to set a 100 mile PR. I passed through 100 miles in 29:34:30, a PR for me by 23 min and 54 seconds.

The longest night passed when an ever so faint pink gossamer broke through the darkness and torched off the sunrise a half hour later.

At sunrise other runners joined in running on the track. Richie got back into the groove again and I approached the 100 mile mark. I decided to get into a wind sprint with Richie at the 99 3/4 mark. We ran the last lap full bore. On the toe off I stressed fractured my third metatarsal bone and had to fall back to a slow walk for the next 9 hours. Other runners joined in and were running at this point. Herb Moriarty (Memphis), Crystal Wilkerson (Memphis) and Pati Baylock (Memphis) had come up with a payment plan for running.

Dave Obelkevich ran with a bizarre kind of obsession through the chill and darkness, keeping a steady pace. A T-shirt did not seem like so big a reward in comparison for the effort he was expending. By the time he had completed the 24 hours he had lapped the track 476 1/2 times. That's 119 miles, 220 yards and there was no prize money for all the mental and physical expenditure these runners had to give on that infinite trail to infinity.

By mid afternoon, the field took on the resemblance of the Battan death march. The runners appeared to have infantile paralysis and crippling MS combined. The frisky lunacy which they started out had become subservient to the sanity of pain and fatigue. Now, it was only survival. There were runners sacked with shades of hypoglycemia, and Jim became like an animal, he bit and snapped at everyone, there was irrationalness in everyone, their minds were not clear—was this a legitimate way to prove their toughness. Richie and I were actually running asleep. The whole lot were chomping on the "ultra bullet," everyone had gone into an oxygen debt so many times they were bankrupted. The needle on their mental tachometers were red scale, they just wanted to go the distance.

A mother and two daughters came over to the track; the mother ran with a beautiful stride and put the ultra runners, in their shuffles to shame. One daughter was wearing gray flannels and on the side it read "no sweat." She did about half a lap and went back and fell into the grass and moaned "this is horrible." Herb Moriarty, Crystal Wilkerson and Pati Baylock and now Becky Vannoy had joined in, they were zooming around the track. Jim Jones and Don Moran ground 62 miles (100KM) and Herb Moriarty ran two back to back marathons for 52.5 miles. Injured Richie Hackney and Crystal Wilkerson ran over a marathon.

At one point, some hippies stood at the edge of the track and puffed on their grass. The runners were getting a bit high on the smoke blowing onto the track and race officials ran the characters out of the field. The ultra-marathon ended at 4:30 p.m. on November 2nd, 1980. Jimmy Robertson had finished in second place with 103 miles to his credit with about 220 yards over. Kevin Donahue broke 100 miles by .4 of a mile to take third place. He ran very steady and has a lot of potential in the future-he's a tough Irishman.

My combined mileage since I started running at the 2.5 mile costume run added up to 109 miles. "I think I have knocked about 9 hours off the 100 mile 60 plus age rating."

I had to do a sub 4 to catch the plane the next day carrying two suit cases and a duffel bag full of running gear. I had my foot in a sling and Gerry was stuffing T-shirts in my brief case; one of them carried the irreverent words, "marathoners keep it up longer."

To all the wonderful and supportive people of Memphis; those who watched the race, worked so hard that others might run, and financed them—"I Love You."

CHAPTER 13

MIDNIGHT SUN RACE ** NORTH POLE

The ultra marathon race started at 7:00 a.m. Four runners lined up at the start line which was also the finish line.

A surprising number of spectators were there to see us off and cameras clicked. Frank Bonzanich, a world class ultra marathoner; Dave Thompson and Marvin Rubinoff, Canadian marathoners and I, were the only runners. We looked at those formidable glaciers, the frozen tundra and roads strewn with boulders and cobblestones. At age 62 it was elbows at the start with guys about half my age.

The starting gun went "Bang" and we took off. Frank Bonzanich set a blistering pace. We all quickly disappeared down the rocky road, dropping about 1500 feet for the next 3 ½ miles; it was called "The crunch" because we had to run it back up again at the finish of the race around the 48 ½ mile mark.

The "Crunch" lasted for about 7 miles after arriving at the loading dock on the sound where the ships take the ore from a storage warehouse about 800 feet long.

I kept zipping up my windbreaker open and shut each time I crested a mountain peak for the wind was blowing strong and cold. The roads were the same as cross country. Sharp gravel, rocks and along the edges the soft tundra (a mossy bog) would feel like running on a continuous inner spring mattress.

I lost no time in forgetting a personal record and decided to "just go the distance." My training for the race had been in a frozen food locker at the local super market, which came in handy. The 30 degree below locker had toughened me to the harsh weather.

Marvin Rubinoff, a dentist from near Toronto, stayed with me for the first 4 miles and then started to burn the course. I let him go, he said later that "he paid for it" by hoofing a lot of miles. There were some very steep downhill runs down mountains on the way to Arctic bay; they were tough on the return trip.

The landscape along the course consisted of eerie blueish rocks, some rusty color and other has purple tint while sill more were steel gray mixed in spooky tints of galena and galvanized zinc mixed with streaks of quartz. The ground seemed one big mammoth rock pile, juxpositioned boulders and some clearings where tundra looked like fine silty green mossy grass dotted with faint purple arctic flowers some looking like small yellow buttercups. Many mountains were in the form of steep fords, plain sheer steep cliffs formed by glaciers centuries ago. The harsh sky seemed filled with billowy clouds, with pink edges and they made the sun fade away minute after minute. The sea seemed to be one huge chunk of ice looking as if it had been hit by a huge explosion and cracked into infinite chunks of ice in a jigsaw puzzle pattern.

As I ran near the sea called Strathcona sound, a lone seal made its way towards the shore and paddled upon the beach, honking its raspy voice, perhaps wondering about the strange runner galloping over the arctic horizon who had dared to invade its sanctuary.

A team of 8 huskies were tired up down the beach, the lead dog was straining against his harness trying to reach the remains of the dead seal about 10 feet in front of him. At about 10 miles I passed three Canadian flags waving from their poles. I said a few prayers to Terry and drank from the jug of ERG mixed with tea Frank had placed there the night before.

I was out about 21 miles when Frank Bozanich passed me. He was on his return marathon about 10 miles ahead of me running up the mountain like a locomotive. Later Dave Thompson passed me; he was nearly 6 miles ahead and Frank was, by now, 6 miles ahead of Dave. Suddenly a bus load of runners passed me in route to Arctic Bay. They shouted cheers and words of encouragement. I still had about a mile and a half on my first marathon when Marvin passed me running his second marathon now about 3 miles ahead of me.

I completed my first marathon coverage at Arctic Bay, it was great! The runners were getting ready to start their marathon in about 25 minutes at 12:30 p.m. Running into Arctic Bay, using my best kick (which was not too fast), I tried to raise my knees higher to make it took like I was going a lot faster.

A lone helicopter flying by twice, someone said he was patrolling for Polar Bears.

After all the rough terrain my flexors were not very flexible, it felt like running on empty. My mental tachometer had been in the red for quite some time. I'd been in so many oxygen debts I was declaring chapter 11. Lactic acid had built up to such a point my beautiful, smooth stride now resembled a silly kangaroo hopping along.

The marathoners suddenly whizzed past me. Robert Russell from Halifax, Nova Scotia led the pack and went on to set a marathon course record of 2:57:41.

At 33 miles out, the unexpected happened. I had a "Blowout." My right sneaker blew out. I had used pneumatic trail winds. I had chosen them because the air was good for insulation and they were comfortable over the sharp stones. I'd worn them over rough terrain before, finding them super on the stones. They absorbed a lot of the shock over the large sized rocks and gave stability on the uneven terrain. The abnormal pronation caused my right foot to lean inwards so the right shoe kept on striking my left ankle bone, causing intense pain. I gutted it out for 11 more miles and one of the fellows at an aid station said he would go back to my room and bring me another pair. Boy, was I surprised when Frank Bonzanich himself jumped out of the vehicle holding my new sneakers. Frank was a great guy. He had won the race in 6:40, a very good itme for an ultra that made the Boston Marathon look like a billiard table. My sneaker blew out on a steep hill which went up about 1,200 feet in five miles. A sign at the start read "The Pain in the Ass." A little later the course took a sudden upturn and the sign at the start read "Marathon Madness." It went up and up! I had used up all my glycogen, fat and had started on my protein. Perhaps a few brain cells were missing by now as well. About 8 miles went by when I passed the village of Nanisivik. Miners, runners and even a few huskies with some Eskimos (Inuit) men and women and also children cheered me on.

The race director, Joe Womersley (Arctic Joe) said I'd better break 12 hours or he's break my neck and leave me in the zinc mine. I just couldn't delay the awards ceremony because I had a parchment scroll for the mayor of Arctic bay, the Nanisivik Mines ltd,. And the Polar Bears Running Club. It was from the Honorable Carl Eilenburg, Mayor of Rome, New York (a running mayor). A veteran runner who'd did a 10 km race by the name of Eric jumped out of a support pickup truck and ran the last mile downhill with me, but he was smart. He didn't run the last 3 1/2 miles uphill called the "Crunch" with me. That was 1500 feet up and over a rough road.

I didn't start my kick until the last KM at about 83.4 KM mark. I put on my "showoff jacket," the one covered with about 70 marathon patches (including 20 ultra marathons). I have been running in the last four years, then I ran "full bore" towards the finish line. My time was 11:53:47, not too bad for an Old man. Dave finished in 9:02:13 and Marvin around 10 hours.

Most of the miners, their families and all other runners had just finished eating their evening meal. Some runners were rubbing their sore limbs and drinking beer at the finish line. They cheered so loud when I ran across the finish line; it felt like I was in a cyclotron!

Joe, the race director, said I was speechless for the first time (I usually talk about 78 RPM). Someone threw me a blanket for my shoulders. I finally muttered something about setting Old Age back at least ten years, but in my heart I knew I'd died a little that day.

CHAPTER 14

1981 MARION CORRIGAN MEMORIAL 24 HOUR SUPER RUN, AUBURN, NEW YORK (NOVEMBER 21-22, 1981)

My wife, Betty, who was also my handler and support crew, Suzette, my Marathon poodle, and me all awoke to a nerve shattering, soul harrowing, ear splitting telephone at 5:00 am. in a room overlooking a huge tropical decorated indoor swimming pool at the Holiday Inn that dreary Saturday morning of November 21, 1981 at Auburn, New York.

We checked out and headed to Friendly's for pancakes. The waitress looked at me in open eyed disbelief as I dumped a pint of liquid fructose on my hotcakes instead of using the maple syrup she shoved at me from across the counter. Little did she realize that I'd run for 24 hours on the goopy glob of griddle cakes saturated in an anemic viscous sticky syrup. She just shook her head in dismay and went after the two cups of black coffee I'd ordered.

Betty took the sausage from her pancakes to our dog Suzette who was waiting in the car with her black leathery nose pressed against the car window and her eyes glued on the front door.

A few minutes later I arrived at Auburn's Cayuga county College Holland quarter mile outdoor field track only to find blizzard like winds screaming through Holland stadium, freezing rains and snow squalls had made the outside event impossible, rain, sleet and snow had filled the pot holes and turned the track into a muddy and slippery track. I was logistically prepared to run in about any weather, but for the sake of spectators, race officials and runners the event was moved indoors on a certified 150 meter metric track while gale force winds with a piercing dampness caused frost bite and hypothermia to be of top concern and made my Gore Tex windbreaker feel more like a palm beach jacket.

The other runners were: Kenny Davis (16), A young man who ran very well and ground out 75.4 miles, he must have slept some during the night because at his speed he would have covered a greater distance. Perry Cook (22), 50.7 miles, bill Reynolds (25), 50.5 miles, Jack Brennen (20), 41.84 miles and the youngest runner Mark Hall (13), who ran 41.75 miles.

The instructions given at the start of the race were quite simple, we'd start at the sound of the gun at approximately 10:20, on Saturday morning and run for 24 hours.

Nine ultra marathoners and a member from the 24 hour relay team all lined up at the start. Suddenly the starting gun sounded and smoke was fanned across the track as Wilson and Hastings, and a runner from the relay team, leaped forward, quickly agitating and dispersing the blue cloud into streamers. Sue was right on their heels, while Perry, Bill, Jack, Kenny, Mark and myself took it a bit easier and just zoomed around the track for that first lap on the oval. I felt just like NASCAR champs: Evans, Waltrip, Foyt, Yarborough, and Andretti all rolled into one just zooming around that track without a motor or wheels in sneakers.

It didn't take me long to realize the pace was too fast. Suzette, my marathon poodle came in and did a couple of laps and quit. Betty brought her back to sign autographs (paw prints) for her fans. I locked in on a pace which would put me at the 50 mile mark in about 10 hours and still allow me for pit stops and time to take short therapeutic walks every 15 minutes to keep my legs from cramping.

The race course was somewhat boring as it took 11 laps to equal one mile. We'd change directions every 2 hours to unwind. The race officials had a big bull horn to give us our instructions with. I didn't mind the short looping track; it seemed to give me further insight in the world of running. I began to wonder if it was a 24 hour exercise in lunacy as one spectator labeled it, to find out what Coe and Scott feel like when they kick around the track. I never appreciated just how fast both Al's and Sue were moving until I suddenly felt their hot breaths on the back of my neck while they whizzed past and kept blowing my arms off as they gained laps on me. But all that would change later when the snowballing lunacy with which they started out with became normalized by the sanity of exhaustion and fatigue.

The public address system blared forth rock and roll music and songs with a good beat to pace one's self by. But after while I suggested they break the record or burn the tape of one hit song named, "Another one bites the dust." that song started to put a psychological whammy on me. Often I'd find my feet actually following the music beat. If they'd played "Flight of the Bumble Bee," "Saber Dance," or the "William Tell Overture," I'd probably blew a racing flat and wound up in an anaerobic mode like a terminal oxygen debt. I recalled in the early morning hours after about 21 hours of hoofing and screeching around the track; those big multi cellular loud speaker quads blasted out with an appropriate Beatle song "It's been a hard day's night." It had a good beat plus the words held a very special significance.

The prime adversaries kept trying to outdo the other, it was truly a grudge run, for awhile it looked like a tossup between the two Al's but by golly Sue was hanging in there running as graceful as a ballet dancer. If she kept it up, those guys would be in trouble. But after 8 hours her legs cramped a bit and her stride became a little ragged. My wife gave her a rub down with some of my powerful analgesic horse liniment, which is also good to clean out the sinuses. That stuff is so powerful it would mollify a petrified hamstring. Sue and I kept cheering each other on, and we even passed encouragement to the leaders, we were all in this thing together. Sue regained her beautiful stride but later was troubled with some general fatigue; but who wasn't. My wife Betty gave Sue massages of her legs with the liniment every two hours until she left at midnight and went to stay with Bill and Sandy Naiva, some wonderful people who gave her a place to sleep and supper. Their son Scott (15) ran in the 24 hour relay for the March of Dimes, which went on simultaneously with the ultra marathon, only they ran in the outer lanes. My marathon poodle, Suzette, managed to get in a minor scrap with their cat and almost had to sleep in the car.

Al Hastings pulled ahead of the pack early but everyone was hoping he'd hit the wall, when he did slow down it was too late for anyone to catch up with him, he was really tough, but his adversary the ex-marine Wilson was perhaps even tougher. He was packing a lot more weight and didn't have the true ectomorphic build that of a racehorse, like Hastings, but he was gutty.

At about half an hour before the closing time of the race I'd gone over 98 miles, many people who had followed the event by local radio (WMBO) and newspaper (The citizen) and other media started pouring into the field house, they were curious about all the excitement and pledging that was going on for the March of Dimes and YMCA fund. These people and friends of the runners all came to see the conclusion of the event. It was a great moment to grandstand if anyone had anything left. I'd sort of waited for this moment. Someone told me to speed up the pace or I wouldn't hit the century mark. The thought of not making it caused a violent reaction. I shouted "illigitimus carborundum" (Latin) for "wear the bastards down" and started doing wind sprints. Someone yelled out, "They don't call that guy "The Incredible Huck" for nothing!" Sadly enough the guy had read his watch incorrectly and there I was doing intervals near the 100 mile mark. By now each foot had struck the tartan track over a 100,000 times. How's that for an overuse syndrome! Remembering the philosophy of Dr. Sheehan "I was becoming the man I would like to be and perhaps, I am. Once my spirit left my body, sat upon a cloud, flew like a kite 'til the thread of life unraveled!" Weird.

Sue said she felt "terrible" but I reminded her of Dr. Sheehan's slogan taken from Coach Percy Cerruty, "if it hurts, make it hurt more." She evidently took the doc's advice as we shall see later. Her father and mother provided constant vigilance and were a great support team They were a nice couple and I thought what it must have been in it for them.

In those latter hours we all must have gone insane. It was unreal; like a whirling dervish and got real hairy. I pushed my body and mind into zones they'd never been before (well recently, at least), I joked my way thru the pain barrier. I told Mark Hall, the youngest runner to keep moving or I'd use him for a "leg transplant." The chair lady for the March of Dimes, Mrs. Eleanor Cook, kept offering her help to see if she could find a new 9 volt battery for my bionic legs, but she handed me a cup of orange juice instead. Near midnight a lady gave me some spaghetti, it gave me a terrible stomach cramp, that spicy sauce in fact my pancreas felt like it had collapsed. I gulped down a handful of dolomite tablets and gutted it out. I ran grotesquely bent forward, just like an attack of scoliosis. Leslie, a young girl from the Auburn High School gymnastic class, ran, jogged and race walked with me for about four hours. We covered about 20 miles from 6:00 to 10:00 p.m., she was like a cheering squad, she would do a complete flip or somersault in the air and land on her feet. Her mother told me that Leslie couldn't get up the next morning, she was pretty beat.

Near the 100 mile mark, I decided to give all the spectators a thrill, I'd burn the course and literally climbed mentally out of my body, got up on my shoulders and booted myself like a jockey, for that sprint I imagined beating myself with a chain, and putting the hammer down by twisting my right hand clockwise to pump more gas into the visionary big Harley motorcycle under me; faster and faster like a kamikaze shouting, kill, kill, kill! My burgundy colored Etonics were just a blur. I went head to head with Dave Hall, a sprinter from the 24 hour relay team, I out kicked him for about 50 meters, but couldn't hold it, and Dave was startled.

By now Mark Hall looked like he belonged in the wheel chair category. My brain, if any, had been disconnected from my body by a special metaphysical process, suddenly I could hear many people cheering as I ran full bore to complete the 100 miles but my day was not yet over. Looking at my watch it looked like 22 minutes remained for me to bite the ultra bullet; my breath was hot as St. George's Red Eyed Apparition, just like a cutting torch. I recall cursing my limitations and then felt silly and started praying for St. Jude to intercede, wondering if my votive candle had gone out in the Vatican.

On and on I ran, seemingly like hours, those last minutes were eternity. But suddenly the crowd went wild, the count down! This was it, the grand finale…"Call In The Clowns" I screamed and pushed thru the barrier for the stunt that would give the crowd a thrill, it was the apex of madness, the sum total of life, the summation of agony, and culmination of pain, the sigma of endurance, I ran like a maniac throwing away all mental crutches. Till I died this stream of memory would set me apart from the world. I'd shared a lifetime of memories in the last day. While the earth had turned only once, I'd run 1.088 laps around the 150 meter metric track, plus another 42.9 meters about (163.24 km) or 101.425 miles (101 miles 754 yards). I'd set a national 24 hour record for the 60 plus bracket age and passed through the 100 mile mark in exactly 23:38:07.56 for another 100 mile national record for the 100 miles. It was a rough training schedule that led up to that race. The weekend before it a 50 mile depletion run at the Nickle City Buffalo run, a 50 miler, plus over 50 miles of training for the week added to the 101.435 miles made it over a 200 mile week. Some kind of training record in itself for a 60 plus runner. In the weeks before I ran Ocean City Marathon at Newport, R.I., the prepaction marathon in Margertsville, New York, the 100 KM AMJA ultra in Chicago on October 4th where I set the national 1981 100 KM RRCA record in the 60 plus bracket and over 20 marathons and ultras for the year dating back to January. In all it was my 76th marathon and 23rd ultra marathon in the past four years. The frost was still on me from running the North Pole Ultra, a double marathon (52.4 miles), 2,000 miles North of Montreal, up where the Polar bear roams, at Nanisivik, at the Northern most tip of Baffin Island (an Eskimo out post in the frozen arctic) on the 5th of July 1981.

Al Hastings had gone on to win the event with 122 miles 528.971 yards, and Al Wilson came in second with 118 miles, 1499.4 yards. Sue finished third with 116 miles, 676.7717 yards to possibly move up to 4th place in the world for her efforts. Ken Davis chalked up 75.4 miles, Perry Cook ran 50.7 miles, Jack Brennan 41.84 miles, Bill Reynolds 50.5 miles and the youngest runner Mark hall cranked out 41.75 miles and got a bit of sleep besides. The event was financially profitable with over $12,000.00 pledged or donated to the sponsors during the 24 hour period.

The real hooker came when I'd finished the race and the race official had set a rubber cone marker down in my footstep at the last second of the race. I then realized I'd pledged a dollar a mile on myself. By wife Betty came over and handed me my check book. After writing out a check for $101.50, I presented it to Mrs. Elanor Cook, chairlady for the March of dimes and the press snapped my photograph of the event. Later I chewed on the microphone for a bit, interviewed by a couple of newspapers and decided not to run a victory lap. All the other runners joined in for a group photograph. I received an AAU/TAC medal, having won the masters category also, and a huge cheese cake which we shared with the Naiva family.

While driving back home on the New York Thruway, my wife said "giving the money to the March of dimes was just great, they will put it to good use in the prevention of birth defects." Later, while staring ahead into the snow squalls, she said, "I know of one person that is suffering from a major birth defect…"Like missing a whole brain." I didn't hear a word. I was wondering if the 24 hour run was going to be enough depletion run for the Philadelphia marathon next weekend.

CHAPTER 15

MONTAUK TO MANHATTEN ** RUNNING ODYSSEY

Drenching rain fell dismally in droplets. Steady and relentless soaking the entire eastern seaboard, as a weather frontal system moved slowly over Long Island.

At 4:00 a.m. that bleak October morning, how depressing to awaken to the annoying chattering alarm clock and hearing the rhythmic, staccato, and the patter of the steady rain falling on the window panes. "The rain storm will only serve to make the challenge greater, I thought, while "gulping down a handful of vitamins, minerals and other ergogenic aids (for this Montauk to Manhattan run I needed all the help I could get from those bio-chemists).

Irene Horn, a member of my support crew arrived and poured black coffee to help synthesize the fatty acids in my blood stream so they could be used for a source of energy before all my glycogen reserves were depleted. I would get 20 miles for free out of that cup of coffee! I knew from experience that this ritual would produce some psychological and synergistic effects, but truly, for long distance running there isn't any subterfuge for a good diet and 100 miles training weeks; plus a marathon or ultra marathon every weekend, with interval training and some hill work thrown in. The only way I had found to strengthen my body was to stress "the hell out of it," and I had been doing a fair job for the past five years with over 100 marathons and 31 ultra races over 50 KM along with literally hundreds of shorter races. I had run equivalent to around the world at the equator in the past six years. I remember driving the uranium spike in the ground celebrating my 24,000 miles last summer.

Now, I recall the mad drive from Stony brook to Montauk Point, during a flash flood, even with the windshield wipers going full blast, the visibility ranged from semi translucent to opaque. The 80 mile grim trip from Stony Brook to the lighthouse, on the tip of Long Island, took one and a half hours. The automobiles looked more like speeding hydroplanes on a vast lake streaking up and down route 27, Montauk Highway. Early bird commuters sought to beat the traffic jams and zoomed along at 5:00 am. while the town's people were still asleep. The refractions of each car and street light caused a glare and transient reflective counterpart of the primary light source which danced blindly upon the wet highway and came to rest in the retinas of my stare.

At 6:30 a.m. I drove past the city of Montauk. The "point," which was my destination, still lay six miles ahead at the extreme eastern tip of Long Island. Suddenly, visible were the thin flashing radians from the multimillion candle power light beam sent from the famous Montauk Point lighthouse, a beacon which had guided ships past that treacherous point since 1796. Every few seconds the revolving light pinnacle pervaded the black night, through fog and rain.

My spirits quickened rapidly as the beacon drew nearer while the road took on a roller coaster like series of inclines and dales. Massive sand dunes had replaced the smooth roads leading to Monauk point. A scant clearing of the sky in the east let in a faint glimpse of dawn; however, the rain persisted. Even the car radio sounded garbled; perhaps the antenna had been grounded out by the flooding conditions.

Upon arriving at Montauk Point in front of the lighthouse, I had hoped to place my foot into the ocean, but a chain link fence, with a padlock on the gate stopped me. It was 7:00 a.m., a member of my crew said "Run for your supper," as the red tail lights of the car dimmed in the fog.

I was all alone, running in the rain. Even with the rain suit on it felt like standing under a shower. After about 100 yards my shoes started "squishing," and became heavier, like weights on each ankle.

Steadily I ran, up and down the sand dunes, toward Montauk. There was no glorious sunrise. The morning went from black to gray and the rain kept pouring. To the right of the macadam road, sea gulls perched on bleached, grey telephone poles.

On I ran, counting the poles and cursing the rain. Then my mind drifted to philosophize upon those amazing birds. My rational being, they have everything going for them. Flying as if they had a built in airplane or magic carpet and floating upon the water in their built in ship, they walk and run the beach. Their eyes are keener than humans, able to spot a minnow from the clouds; their ears can hear the faintest squeak. They make their own kind, and others understand their attitudes with squaks (language enough). They are not concerned with clothing or shelter. Gulls keep warm and dry with their feathers that let the rain drip off and they keeps out the cold. They do not need cars or supermarkets. God designed them wonderful and functional. Man has fouled up their environment. I have seen them hitchhike three thousand miles over the ocean on the mast of a ship and still return to their homes; some gyro compass they have built in and they do not pay rent or income taxes.

Every gull gawked at me as I ran along the solitary highway, perhaps feeling superior, but only interested in food for its gizzard. One gull seemed a little more energetic and adroit, much like Jonathon Livingston, and did a few dapper dives while flying off to the nearby beach to look for some food washed ashore from a garbage scowl. Oddly, the destruction of the marine life and plants has driven them to become scavengers and it now seems to be only a matter of time when the polluted seas and land will drive them to extinction. Strange analytical thoughts were coming from my oxygenated brain.

The scrubby trees along the roadside were hardwood, and greens. The hardwoods were now in full color as autumn had reached its peak. Ranging in hues from vermillion for the maples to cadmium yellow mixed with orange tints of golden shades, drab browns, ochers and seanas for those soggy leaves fallen upon the ground.

The salt air drove the rain into occasional showers as I ran past Montauk towards East Hampton, passing by Hither Hills State Park.

East Hampton was reached at 10:00 a.m., I had covered the route in the rain, now the rain had given away to a beautiful sunny day. I spotted a coin operated Laundromat near the road and hurried over to dry my wet soggy clothing. I ran into the Laundromats rest room and shed my dripping clothing and tossed them out the door to the attendant who stuffed them into the dryer, shoes and all, then I spent the next half hour in the "john" waiting for them to dry out.

Back on the road again, I picked up the pace while concentrating on the marathon mile markers along the route that someone had painted on the highway. I had followed the mile markers which started at Montauk, all the way through Bridgehampton and Water mill, to the intersection of routes 27 and 27A. I recall passing the 25 mile mark but never saw the 26 mile mark (I assumed it went into South Hampton). At the junction, route 27 made a 90 degree bend to the right. I followed the iron guard rails. In Bridgehampton I met a fellow riding a Lotus bike, his name was Tom O'Conners, he said he was a sprinter but had run some marathons, and told me he was working the finish line of the New York Marathon to throw the unofficial runners out of the chute.

Five miles past Southampton rout 27 changed into a four lane, divided highway and another three miles further along I ran over Shinnecock canal which connects the Great Peconic Bay to Shinnecock Bay. On the bridge I found an 18 inch monkey wrench weighing about five pounds. I carried it along with me as I ran, several miles further down the road I passed the city of Hampton Bays, so far I had covered 42 miles in the last 8 hours and still had two and a half hours of daylight left. I lost my small map which I carried from the start. I remember passing Speonk Riverhead road (route 88) but did not see any more towns for a long time. Finally I stopped at a diner and called my support crew to pick me up.

We arrived close to 9:00 p.m. I had eaten a large plate of spaghetti. After two cups of coffee we returned to Stony brook. Stage I was completed. I had covered over 100 kilometers in 13 hours and 29 minutes. I was averaging 4.6 mph. The rain and time spent drying my clothing had hurt my average, my pace had been at 6 mph, with occasional brisk walks to keep my legs from cramping.

A nerve shattering, soul harrowing, ear splitting alarm clock awoke me at 5:00 a.m. Shortly, I was eating breakfast and by 6:30a.m. I was running. My support crew had dropped me at the diner near Shirley on route 27A. I remember running through the city of Patchogue and in downtown Sayville. The sunrise peeked over St. Lawrence, the Martyer Catholic church; the church had yellow brick with a dark brown roof constructed in two dark brown truncated geometric hemispheres and a similar spire. At the spires apex a small wire like cross glistened while silhouetted against the huge red fireball sun which slowly rose in the southeast. The temperature was hovering near freezing, my hands became numb. I did not have gloves on so I took of my socks and put them on my hands and ran without socks on my feet. I am an engineer and it seemed the most logical thing to do.

On my right I passed a clear lake; seven ducks including two green headed Mallards, were swimming about. On the distant shore stood a flock of large white birds, a beautiful white swan glided along in the middle of the lake. The early morning sun shone on the tiny ripples making the water appear like a sea of shimmering gold. Three miles past Oakdale, Route 27A (which was hilly and had narrow hazardous bridges) intersected route 27.

The millions of automobiles traveling this major highway over the years had littered the roadside with every imaginable fragment of rubbish. I passed two dead cats hit by cars, a long tail mouse and enough tools and wrenches to start up a garage business. I found over $7.00 in change along the route. At one place money was all mixed with cigarette butts and I assumed someone dumped their ash tray (that had coins stuffed in it) out their car window. It was truly a study in ecology. There was a maintenance crew of six men equipped with poles out fitted with sharp spikes on the ends were cleaning the highway. They were following a large yellow state truck with black cross hatchings. I noticed one of the workers had speared a pair of women's nylon silk underpants. I stopped and asked him if he found many panties along such a busy highway. "I find girls panties in all sizes and colors," he replied. I told him out here on a four lane highway; it did not make any sense with all the hotels, houses, motels and resorts all over the island, and asked him what he thought. "They just can't wait" was his reply. A Street cleaning vehicle with big revolving brushes came by and 1 ran behind it until I realized it was plugging up my lungs. There were more tools lying in the breakdown lane, but I did not pick them up, that five pound monkey wrench I ran with for 20 miles the day before had taught me a lesson.

About noon I reached Massapequa. I had gone approximately 30 miles in the past 6 hours, running through towns of Patchogue, Sayville, East Islip, West Babylon and Lindenhurts on the way stopped at a diner and ate a diet plate consisting of fresh fruit and cottage cheese. It was a good choice as it did not upset my stomach. The worst thing I ate was bacon and eggs that morning. My advice is to stick with pancakes without any bacon, ham or sausage. The meat and grease gave me the "burps" for over 20 miles.

I recall passing through the cities of Wantagh, Merrick and finally reaching Lynbrook at 4:00 p.m. I had run nearly 50 miles in nine and one half hours, but the weather was perfect and I only had a ten minute delay to eat dinner. I had averaged 5 ¼ miles per hour.

After passing Valley stream the traffic became heavier towards the JFK International Airport. The neighborhood began to look pretty rough going towards East New York and some kid threw an orange at me half moldy green from decay. I decided I'd had it for the day and ran back towards Valley Stream and called Harvey, my support crew, to pick me up. He said to head north and call him back. I telephoned him from South Jamaica on Merrick Blvd. Harvey had to work overtime and did not pick me up until 6:00 p.m. I had run close to 60 miles in eleven and a half hours, but the course was flat, very few small inclines, not enough to notice. I was still about eleven miles short from finishing my run to Staten Island and decided to run it on Saturday evening. Harvey took me back to Stony Brook where I met Irene's daughter Janice and her husband and daughter 8 months old who played the baby part of Little Gloria in the story of Gloria Vanderbilt, a recent TV feature movie.

On Saturday, Dr. Augustus "Gus" Prince, A scientist and marathoner from Brookhaven Labs, joined us. I put him on my support crew as technical advisor. He provided some sound concepts about the phosphates from skim milk triggering the ADT (Adenosine Triphosphate) molecules in my leg muscles and making them twitch and suck up more glycogen and some advanced Krebs cycle aspects. I was hoping for something more positive, like sticking my legs in his Van Der Graff generator and recharging them.

The news media had gotten hold of my epic run and I received several telephone calls regarding the endurance feat. The New York Times and others carried the story from interviews made with me.

Saturday afternoon I returned with Harvey to finish stage 3 of my Trans Long Island plus New York marathon run. Irene decided to run the last twelve miles with me and Harvey would provide support facilities, driving about half a mile ahead and waiting for us. Irene was no slouch of a runner and had some fast 10K, 15K and 10 mile times and was in the top 5 in her age category in the 1982 National running Data center. It was a good thing I had a hundred and twenty miles warm up because she ran like a ballet dancer, pushing sub eight minute miles. As we ran across Brooklyn we met two of the cutest black children, like flower people. I gave them an autographed, photograph with my life story on the back and they seemed so grateful. After about 7 miles Irene slowed a bit and I tried some coaching, I sang the Star spangled Banner, told her she was running for the Olympic gold, the Russians were behind her, and sang an aria from the Opera La Traviata which caused her to really pick up the pace as we ran over the Verranzano Bridge. Harvey was waiting for us; he pulled the car off the road near the toll booths, and took our pictures. It was dark about 7:00 p.m. and the traffic was heavy. We had run the first 13.1 miles in 2 hours and 4 minutes. My cumulative run time 27 hours 13 minutes for a distance of 134.3 miles or a 4.9 mile per hour average. My Montauk Point to Staten Island leg of the run was now complete.

My crew and I left for New York City Chinatown for a Chinese dinner of rice and vegetables. I figured if Chinese people can work all day at hard labor in the fields on just a bowl of rice, it should get me through the New York City marathon tomorrow.

While waiting, standing in line in front of the restaurant I met Liz Elliott, Executive director, of the American Running and fitness association. She remembered me from way back in 1979 when the National Jogging Association voted me "Jogger of the Month" for May, 1979.

At the Chinese restaurant my thoughts were filled with plans on how to bring to the attention of the millions of people watching the race in person and perhaps nationwide television a new dimension to running. To the majority of spectators, running 100 KM or 62 miles day after day was unheard of. The limit of their running concepts were restricted to the standard 26.2 mile marathon they had watched year after year. Ultra marathoning and stage races were unknown to most of them. When millions of people read of my running oddesy in the New York Times, they would be looking for me, trying to pick me out among the 16,000 runners. Because my epic run was not associated with the New York Marathon except I would follow the last 26.2 miles of blue line, it seemed best to really stand out. Therefore, rather than run with the pack and end up obscure with terminal claustrophobia, I would start two hours earlier and hope to finish before the lead runner of the marathon could pass me. I would carry some autographed photos with my life's story on the back and a few resumes, for my fans. It would be necessary to wear my show off jacket with the marathon patches on it, a bright red jacket with my name printed in 3 inch high letters "Incredible Huck" on the back of the jacket for positive identification. "This odyssey will literally traumatize the spectators," I thought as I bit into a fortune cookie.

Harvey, an amateur radio operator, assigned to the ten mile mark of the New York City marathon, had to be on station before 9:00 a.m. on race day. He drove me over the Verrazano Bridge, went through the toll gate and came back through the other side. Seemingly hundreds of policemen with sticks wearing black leather jackets guarded the area. I told Harvey to drive fast up to the marathon start line and I would jump out and start running over the bridge. I was really getting nervous; most of those cops were big and looked like they really meant business. However, they did not expect a sneak attack from the front, I'd caught them off guard and had a good two hundred yard head start before they started running my way but the bridge is up hill and they could see it was too late for a Keystone Kops routine. At that point I was running under a seven mile minute pace on a ledge about 18 inches wide. Some traffic still came through so it was dangerous in case I got off balance. Then, came the most frightening maneuver of all. At the location of the giant suspension trestle of reinforced concrete, the narrow cat walk I ran on narrowed out in half by the juxpositioned protruding concrete slab, with the traffic leaving turbulent storm like wakes and contrails of monoxide, making my legs shaky. I inched along like Spiderman, grasping the cement wall with the flat palms of my hands. It must be over a hundred feet across this obstruction and after what seemed like hours I made it clear. I was spotting the winner two hours and knew I would have to run perhaps under 4:08 to beat him. I had a 135 mile warm up and had lost about 10 pounds to 147.

Over the Verrazano Bridge I picked up a blue stripe marking the course that I would follow to the finish line as long as possible. My red show off jacket, with the maze of marathon/ ultra marathon patches, felt good as the temperature was in the high 30's and the wind blowing briskly giving a bad chill factor.

Upon reaching Fourth Avenue, in Brooklyn, I was surprised to find the streets already filling with spectators at a little after 9:00 a.m. Some asked me why I was running so soon. I told them I was on a Montauk Point to Manhattan running Odyssey, so with all the professional looking equipment, jacket and muscle sculptured legs they sensed I was for real and cheered me on.

I remember passing the five mile marker shortly before 67th street. My watch showed my average was 8.5 pace having run it in just under 43 minutes. A few Hasidic Jews wearing black hats, coats and white shirts with ties stopped momentarily to ponder my antics. But strangely several observers in every block recognized me as they had apparently read the New York Times that morning, which told of my epic run. The further I ran the more people recognized me. I passed through ten miles in 83 minutes. Harvey was there at the marker with his two meter amateur rig caught up in the net control circuit solving an unbelievable number of logistic problems, like how do you mix ERG? He called the manufacturer, using phone patches, etc., and got the answer. They also had a problem with some of the carpeting that had been stolen off the Queensboro Bridge. Around Greenpoint Avenue I ran a block out of the course way when a photographer running backwards took my picture, he was clicking away and ran backwards over the bridge on McGuinnes Boulevard over a small river going into the East River just before 49th street.

People were now out by the millions. The official start of the 1982 New York City Marathon was in progress. There wasn't any more time to lose, if I did not want a repeat of the 1982 Boston Marathon where Salazar and Beardsley blew my arms off near the chute at Boston, I'd have to go for it. At the 15 mile marker the race officials told me to get a move on and filled up my water container. I was using a bicycle water bottle and ran with it stuffed in the back waist of my running shorts. One official further adding a contrapuntal after though that the TV cameras were waiting for me, along with the press at the Tavern on the Green in Manhattan's Central Park.

They had replaced the stolen carpet on the Queensboro Bridge and I ran inspired by the crowd's enthusiasm. The crowds along the way numbered over two million, now cheering spectators lined the route. The crowd really got me going, there could be no "wall" for me with that kind of mob. The temperature felt about 15° with the wind chill factor, where in reality, it must have been about 45. The thrill of personal victory caused me to roar thru the Queens. I remember they had a lot of oranges near Rascals Bar on Manhattan's Eastside when running up First Avenue, I recall the route at near 19 miles entered the south Bronx. It took me 3 hours plus to reach the 20 mile marker. I would have to hold the same pace to beat the winner to the finish line. I kept counting my left foot strikes to check my pace, it was right on, but for the first time my stride was harder to hold. Reaching out now my hands touched the palms of dozens of little children, hopeful that some of their youthful energy would be synthesized and transcend into my hamstrings. Some of the tiny hands seemed to zap me, perhaps hunger, strife, and unhappiness had developed negative minds. "Yet others seemed to radiate positive feelings which when added in tandem with my own energies caused an ethereal sensation of floating crossed the Harlem River and headed towards the Central Park entrance at 102nd street and Fifth Avenue. From the sound of the choppers I could now hear and information I gathered from the portable radios, the lead runners Salazar and Gomez were about half way up First Avenue about 18 miles into the race. My run through Central Park was filled with fear, the lead runners were closing in and my anxiety grew as the police struggled to keep the crowds back. They did not bother me; I broke into an 8 minute pace and ran like a possessed Wildman amuck. I could not believe it, with one mile still to go, the lead runners had entered the park, my fears were made manifold, hundreds of policeman now struggled to hold back the wild crowds now, many thought I was the winner, one little boy said, "Look at that old man run." Still the police did not throw me off the course. Suddenly, I reached Central Park Square; just around the corner was the chute. Only 385 yards to go…this…was it…a sprint. I had reached the 160th mile of my 4 day running odyssey.

Half a mile back Salazar and Gomez were dueling it out. Suddenly the biggest cop I ever saw jumped out in front of me. To escape him I ran into the unofficial runners chute…into oblivion. I sprinted beside the crowd behind the bleachers, on past the finish line, and waited for the winners. The clock read 2:08:27 (my marathon time was 4:08:27). One minute later I saw Salazar break the ribbon at 2:09:29 then Gomez crossed four seconds later, at 2:09:33.

It was a captive audience. Millions of people drawn on the streets by the New York City Marathon.

Next time instead of running from Montauk Point, I will be on a 3,542 mile, 77 day running odyssey from Los Angeles to Manhattan, but my timing will be better; hopefully arriving at least an hour before the marathon winner hits the tape, running Odyssey #2. "Huck's run."

CHAPTER 16

THE FIRST
60KM CANANDAIGUA LAKE FALL CLASSIC "A DEVIL OF A GOOD RUN"

The first Canandaigua Lake Classic, a 60 KM (37.3 mile) ultra marathon, a fund raiser listed as a "Run for Hope" for the American Cancer Society and sponsored by the Finger Lake Enterprise of Penfield, New York was run on October 3, 1982.

I learned of the race at the Old Forge Marathon, during the awards ceremony, while scratching through several stacks of race entry sheets. My attention suddenly focused on a yellow-orange colored entry form with a line drawing depicting two large hills and the Devil himself; pitchfork in hand, horns and barbed tail emerging from between the Alps. Printed beneath the cartoon was the following caption, "A Devil of a Good Run." The course circumnavigated the perimeter of Lake Canandaigua about one and a half miles across and about 17 miles long.

I'd become bored with running measly ole standard marathons, having finished one every weekend for the past six weeks. Now, my evangelistic spirit was ready to exercise a devil from his hilly haunts.

On the eve of the race, my wife, Betty and I celebrated her birthday at Rome Post 2246 VFW dinner-dance held to honor N.Y. State VFW commander Voss. I forewent the usual pre race pasta blast and decided to test out Manhattans, as a substitute for spaghetti, and disco vs snoozing. As a self styled vegan I looked glumly at the giant steak and half chicken and dumped it in a doggie bag for Suzette, my marathon poodle. After only one Manhattan (that stuff smells like shoe polish). I needed ankle weights to keep my feet on the dance floor; that drink undone six months of hard Olympic type training.

The alarm clock sounded like a "fire gong" at 2:00 a.m. I crammed down a double handful of vitamin tablets in my mouth; their contents would take at least 6 pages to list; also several garlic parsley caps, which gave me the sour burps for the next two days. I ate some oatmeal hoping it would give me the speed of a race horse, and some banana for the strength of a gorilla.

I scraped the frost from the car windshield, the chilly night wind made my windbreaker feel more like a palm beach suit. I took the New York thruway and arrived at the city of Canandaigua at 5:00 a.m. The only place being open was the Sheraton Motor Inn. The lady at the desk gave me directions and a map to the starting line, but added a contrapuntal after thought which jolted my mind when she said "I hate to drive my car over that route because the radiator always boils over," at that I used the rest room, an architectural marvel, sparkling porphyry china, no poison ivy.

At 6:00 a.m. the runners started showing up in the parking lot, which was the front lawn of the yacht club.

7:00 a.m., at the starting whistle, 17 runners toed the line, Nedra Weaver and a girl from the relay team were the two women represented. Everyone took off all set on chasing Satan out of the hills. I had to eat those garlic caps three times in the first mile.

The sun came slowly up from across the lake, just like a big fried egg, while its rouge gossamers rippled to the shore; sail boats were already cruising along the chill breeze caught their nylon gibs. I didn't see anything that looked like a demon, a glorious sunrise, the awe stricken splendor of autumn, only God's handiwork prevailed. The leaves were at their peak colors. Ranging in hues from vermillion for the Shumac, to cochineal, chromate and cadmium yellows mixed with orangish tints amid burnished golden luster's for the Maples. The small byzantine shaped elm foliage being the lesser brilliant, with drabs of earth tones of raw and burnt siennas and umbers.

rse was easy for the first five miles, at which point demon mountains set in, a two mile grade of over 1,000

...ingly infinite asfault and macadam roads interfaced with rock strewn eroded shoulders. I had to tread gingerly over the rubble when ever a large vehicle crowed me off the shoulder.

All conceivable shades of greens blothed the landscape in variegated chromas from emerald to olive. Furtile orchards ran parallel with the course only disrupted occasionally by a vast vineyard bespecklet with deep purple concord, pale toukeys, and greenish Thompson seedless varieties. Actually, we were running through the heart of the New York wine country. Grapes for sale signs appeared along the course, and Cortland and spy gold apples overfilled bushel baskets. I grabbed a bunch of grapes out of a drainage ditch and popped a few as I ran down route 21 south. A lady pulled along side and from the window of her blue chevy yelled, "they will give you the runs." "Great," I yelled back misinterpreting the verb. Later I picked an apple from a draping tree over the highway. It tasted a lot better than the junk we get in the supermarkets.

Ed Cohn was giving the devil a run for his money and left him in an oxygen debt at the marathon mark, as he blew thru in a surprising fast time of 2:47 and ran over two demon mountains of over 1,500 feet elevation gain doing so. Twenty three minutes later, Bob Russell left his waffle sole prints on the devil laying in the middle of the road and before he could recover, Bill Piper and Tim Youngs running neck to neck trampled him some more again. Walt Connoly, the 52 year old wonder, stomped him soundly at a point 13 minutes later at 3:30, then a whole gang of runners stamped satan including Greg Helbig, Charlie Sabatine, John Kerr, Tom Burt, Steve Vargo, Don Osborne and then Nedra Weaver ran down his back with her new Saucony's leaving their imprints on his rump. The "back of the packers" tromped him some more as Norm Frank, James O'Leary, Bill McCarthy, Mel Olkowski (the Adirondack wolfman) and I sent him back to hades.

I caught the wolfman at the 32 mile marker and he was still running strong, he had a couple of allergy attacks back at 20 miles and we got into a "bull" session. The temperature was up to 70 degrees, but cloud cover kept the afternoon sun out, after being scorched at noon.

There was excellent support to all entries, even the stragglers were well taken care of. Several cars were deployed along the route and plenty of water was available every two miles. Every mile marker was plainly visible in foot high yellow numerals, although they seemed to get further apart towards the marathon mark. Large yellow arrows painted on the roads directed the runners past any wrong turns. Don Williams, the race director, had done, in conjunction with his race officers and helpers, a tremendous job. I believe this race will grow in popularity in the next year and there afterwards and the pledges go for a very worthy cause.

Some lady drove up alongside of me and said she heard about it on the radio. I was about 31 miles out; she parked her car, jumped out and asked me if she could give me a big kiss. I wiped off a little sweat and she gave me a shot of slightly used oxygen.

The lady and her husband who were running the relay finished the race, each doing about half of it or 30 K each.

Wolfman (got his name doing research on wolves back in the Adirondack Mountains at Lake Placid) had a deep scar on his right arm. He'd been hit by a car while riding his bike. We decided to kick it in for a tie, and kicked it in breaking thru a reconstructed red and while ribbon, then headed for the picnic grounds on the campus of the Finger Lakes community college.

Mel told me he's rode on a bus for 10 days going out to Utah and ran in a 100 miler, I think it was the Wasatch trail run, but got lost and ended up with a DNF. I remember last month he'd run from Lake Placid to Star Lake, some 72 miles to run the Adirondack Marathon the next day. He's a running personality.

We learned that Ed Cohn, from the Rochester track club has gone on to win the race. Bob Russell, runner up with Bill Piper taking the 3rd spot. Tim Youngs hung in for 4th and Walt Connoly (52) took the masters. Nedra Weaver in her new saucony's blitzed the course in 6:11:00 for a great effort. The other runners finished pretty much in the same order as they were at the marathon, except Grey Helbig moved ahead of Charlie Sabatine and out distanced him by almost 15 minutes for an excellent 6th place. I finished the race in a tie with a time of 8:26:40 with wolfman.

Race director, Ron McWilliams, expressed pleasure as all the starters finished the grueling race.

In all, you might say, "it was a devil of a good run." See you at the second running of the Canandaigua Lake fall classic 60 Klicker.

This is a portrait I painted of one of my dearest friends

CHAPTER 17

NOVEMBER 7, 1982
ERIE CANAL RUN 60KM

The Syracuse track club (STC) held the first annual 60 km Erie Canal run on November 7, 1982. The run coordinator was Wayne Mydlinski of Syracuse.

The adventure stated at 8:00 a.m. at the Erie Canal park in Syracuse about 2 miles northwest of Fayettville under ideal conditions. A light frost had fallen and the temperature, at the start, read 37 degrees, under clear skies. The finish line being the historic Erie Canal Village in Rome, New York.

Five runners including Wayne, Peter Monteleone, Ewin "Scott" Love, Ed Seeley, Jim McKeever and I showed up to run the towpath. Bob Daley drove the support vehicle to provide aid. It would travel back and forth between the lead runners and the stragglers. The sixth runner, Bill Kissane, wearing a Baltimore marathon T-shirt arrive late and caught us at the 3 mile marathon marker.

I'd lived alongside the Erie Canal for the last 23 years and had been intrigued by it's history. The thought of running about 40 miles along the towpath and studying its construction, plus observing the villages along the way and meditating on life 165 years ago, before man had conquered the skies, the automobile was unheard of, before the discovery of the modern nuclear war missiles; in the days when men ran to save their scalps rather than for sport.

My friend Pete Monteleone (46), a good master marathoner showed up for the event and I was glad to see him. He would run my race pace and I'd be able to keep up with him and the group for at least 10 miles. We ran at about an 8 minute pace at the start. I ran beside Ewin "Scott" Love, English teacher and girls cross country coach and listened to the conversation of the front runners. Bill Kissane, Jim McKeever, another English teacher and cross country coach were discussing running on the track and they were feeling let down over their 4:17 mile. I was traveling in "fast company" but they didn't seem to be in a big hurry. We all took a water break together at the 5 and 10 mile markers.

As I ran along the gravelly towpath the significance of the gigantic canal undertaking really began to hit me. The trees on either side now were like tall gray poles with stragley limbs, a few autumn leaves remained, the last fading remains of pre annual gaudiness. Suddenly like a vision, more facts started filling my thoughts as my feet pounded the path shielded by fallen leaves protecting them from larger stones randomly mixed with sod and dirt.

I tried to recall what little information I'd remembered about the Erie Canal since the digging was begun in Rome, New York. I knew it was 262 miles long and had 83 locks. For every foot I ran someone originally dug the ditch by hand, and piled the dirt up here on the bank (towpath).

On July 4, 1817 in Rome, Revolutionary war veteran, Judge Joshua Hathaway, the first postmaster, turned over the first spade full of earth. At that time it was called "Clinton's Ditch," so named after DeWitt Clinton, twice governor of New York State (1817-23 and 1825-28)

In a dream like trance I saw the barge mules straining against their sweat soaked leather traces. Dragging their west bound cargo along the last stretch of the canal. The mules kicking up puffs of brownish dust and the skinners fore and aft caught up in the slow loping rhythm of the mules in a song on the canal.

I chanced again to see Governor Clinton from aboard the canal boat "Seneca Chief" dumping a cask of pure Lake Erie water into the briny waters of the Atlantic Ocean in the grand ceremony which opened the Erie Canal, and led to a new era in transportation for the next 50 years. It stimulated commerce along its banks and found a place in song, story and legend.

what kind of humans could have dug this ditch I thought? It was hard to believe that 2000 emigrants form...lated by cheap whisky, drunken freely as water, working 12 hours a day and undoubtedly another 6 hours...ld have built such a canal. Armed with pick and shovel and bone-muscle, born of the peat bogs and green ...u of the countries of Cork and Clare, they inched their way through soil, across creeks and field, through rock, sand and swamps as they moved ever westward. Little wonder the hard working and hard living Irish claim they "clawed" out the canal with their bare fingers and then filled it with their sweat.

Pete and I were working up a "bit of sweat" ourselves as the run became more exciting with each mile. We reached Chittenango 13 miles out after 2 hours of running. At 16 miles we were delayed waiting for the New York Central train to pass with about 200 freight cars. At 17 miles, in Canastota, I gassed up on ERG but Pete stuck to water.

Pete was running much stronger than me and he kept running back to check on my progress. We passed Wampsville at the 20 mile mark in just over 3 hours. We ran on to the town of Durhamville, the 24 mile marker, and passed the marathon point at state bridge, just north of Oneida near 5 hours.

Pete invited my attention to a village near New London called Poverty flats. A few more overseas ultras and it may well be my next address. At the 35 mile mark we passed through East Verona.

Previously the sun's reflections on the canal shimmered from towpath to heel path (opposite shore). The sun had disappeared at noon, as a cloudy sky blew overhead.

As I continued to run my technical mind started working with the rhythm of my feet. Sometimes the towpath would change sides, it was then I started to muse on the two to three horses pulling a canal boat, hooked to it with a long rope, changing sides. There was always a bridge which we walked over and a ramp we run up, and another ramp we ran down when the towpath changed sides. I started thinking what a tough job the driver must have had, harnessing, feeding the horses and mules and himself; he walked with one hand on the tow line and the other holding the team's reins for 10 to 15 miles in 6 hours in the hot sun, rain, snow, mud or dark rainy nights. Then he'd feed, unharnessed and eat before he could go to bed. He must have walked in his sleep. My running seemed a picnic compared with that.

Once I saw a box with a long handle on it and its purpose was to plaster dung on the bottom of the outside of the canal boat to stop leaks. They didn't have scuba divers; things must have been really primitive 150 years ago.

The lead group composed of Mydlinski, Love and Seeley had taken a wrong turn at New London and we were gaining on them Pete and I, but not enough, 2 miles from the finish line I met them coming back towards Syracuse. They stopped and gave me the last quart of ERG. Wayne had decided to call it quits about 36 miles, getting off course, psyched him out. I learned also that Kissane and McKeever stopped at Canastota and ran back to their cars at the start line.

We passed Fort Ricky Game Farm on the left where deer and wild animals were well taken care of in a natural habitat setting. A few miles further I passed the automobile museum where some of the older cars of the past are displayed. At the next opportunity I'll check out the museum.

We arrived at historic Erie Canal village in Rome. An authentic reconstructed village built on the land which saw the excavation for the start of the canal. I could not forget how the Irish dug the canal. As they took their places in the ditch they noticed barrels carefully placed at measured intervals along the route. They were not ordinary barrels, but full of whiskey. As the Irish dug their way to a barrel, drained it, then moved on to the next and next until they reached Buffalo.

I sprinted across Rome's Erie Canal village finish line. The run took me 6:55:47 to complete. Pete and his wife were waiting for me with a cold beer. I drank it down in one swig.

Those Irishmen were, pretty smart. After 12 hours on the rip-rap they needed something a bit stronger than beer.

Erie Canal Run

	Run Results	Age	Time
1.	Ewin "Scott" Love	26	5:58:21
2.	Edward "Ed" Seeley	29	5:58.21
3.	Pete Monteleone	46	6:46:34
4.	John Huckaby	62	6.55:47

John's Memorabilia

Location:
Rome Sports
Hall of Fame
Size 6' x 10'

CHAPTER 18

JOHN HUCKABY'S HEARTATTACK

May 15, 1983. My heart faltered at about a hundred yards short of the finish line while running the Ottawa Canada International marathon. Two nurses passing by saw my shoes sticking out of a ditch. They found me with no heart beat and not breathing. I was clinically dead. They administered CPR to no avail. A team of paramedics nearby rushed to the scene and administered the defribulator paddles and my heart began beating and my breathing resumed. Thus my running career was finished.

I awoke in the Ottawa hospital and the beautiful scenes I had when I was clinically dead were like looking through a kaleidoscope. They were replaced by several nurses all wearing pink dresses. I realized I was not in heaven because if they had been in white dresses I would have been looking for wings!

It was time for me to use another gift that God had given to me. Instead of pounding the earth with my feet, I was to caress the canvas with my brush. I looked out the hospital window and gazed at the beautiful landscape and vowed to God to use the remaining days of my life to glorify the Lord. I have kept my promise and glorified God in dozens of paintings and large murals. It was a test for my self actualization to be fulfilled.

God was with me for giving me new life to paint. However, God did not want me to run ever again. I lost one of my three coronary arteries and nearly a half of my heart muscle was replaced by scar tissue that is much weaker than muscle.

Ten years later in August 1993 the two remaining coronary arteries became 95% plugged and I was rushed to Albany, NY medical center for bypass surgery. I remained on a restricted activity program and in the year 2002 I was outfitted with a pacemaker/defribulator. In the year 2006 the manufacture had a recall and I was outfitted with a new device implant. Recalls that started with the automobile industry seem to never end. The doctor advises me that if it beeps at 10 a.m. to rush to Syracuse, NY for a check or replacement.

I hope to quickly after my last breath, "To cross the finish line in heaven."

Following Jesus is the greatest heart run. In my running days there were a lot of hurdles but I have jumped over them with his help. My running with Jesus has had a lot of rewards. So when I finish the heavenly race and hear those angels cheer, and Jesus puts a golden crown upon my head, I'll give him praise and thanks.

Book Eight

CHAPTER 19

ELECTRONIC ADJUNCT MOHAWK VALLEY COMMUNITY COLLEGE 1960

I taught the advanced course in electronics for two semesters at MVCC Utica, NY during the evening class, a 28 mile trip. There were about 20 students who had theory and hands on training. It was a very gratifying teaching position and my students went on to become very successful in the electronic and communication field. I gave the students lessons needed to obtain a FCC license. The pay was seven dollars a week which didn't cover the cost of the gasoline for the trip.

JOHN'S VENTURE INTO THE BUSINESS WORLD 1961-1989

I attended MVCC at Utica NY for two years taking business courses; the classes were in the evenings and taught by highly skilled business men. My wife and I had purchased several mobile homes and multifamily apartments and houses we rented. It became obvious that to be highly successful it would be necessary to gain some business education. Therefore I took every available subject related to management and money. For example, accounting, real estate and appraising, financial management, business management, and interior decorating. My wife Betty had graduated in book keeping, typing, shorthand and writing in addition she help supervisory and filing and taking dictation at fast and accurate speed. She was just the perfect person to be a landlord, not gullible, business like and straight forward and decisive. We were a team!

We put down a couple thousand dollars and bought a small piece of land and had some development and rapidly expanded it by renting, high enough above the mortgage to quickly own the rental. It wasn't tong before we had a roof over a hundred peoples heads. It wasn't all a piece of cake. We still had a lot to learn.

In 1970 we entered the manufactured homes sales in our spare time until 1978. We sold our resort park middle July 1982 and moved into our apartment house. I retired from civil service January 2, 1986 and 1989 we bought our present home and have lived there since, to the present date 2011.

HUCK'S REALESTATE

I was always thinking of writing a book about real estate, however instead of titling it "How I made a million in real estate" he had often thought a more appropriate title would have been "How I lost my (a picture of a donkey should be inserted here) in real estate." After going to college at night for over seven years just studying business which included, industrial management, commercial law, accounting, stocks and bonds, real estate I and II and real estate appraising, and several other coruses in banking and money subjects finally concluding his education in the financial world with interior decorating which proved quite expensive to him before he could make things look pretty but others could make them into a dump in just a day or so.

While in real estate school in college I had this professor who was a lawyer, clear title and do the necessary legal paper work so he could get a deed which was called "fee simple absolute" in legal terminology. The ideal investment was a five family apartment house which was badly in need of repairs, the tenants were too poor to move and most of the income came from social service checks, the apartments were always rented as I did not try to make a profit beyond my depreciation schedule, and I had to pay the mortgage, taxes, water, electric and all the repairs. The biggest expense seemed to be paint Every time some new tenant moved in they never liked the paint job the last tenant put on, the colors were always mismatched regardless of who decorated the apartment.

The years to come found me involved with some of the most unusual types of humanity. The first minority group that shocked my faith in my human brotherhood of man was the hippies. After fighting for rents for about 5 years during the early part of the sixties, one day a clean shaven man with a nice car drove up and rented the nice middle apartment. The fellow had a college degree and seemed above the usual rif-raf that I had spent a small fortune in lawyer's fees to evict over the years. The fellow proved to be the real antichrist. Within a weeks time the metamorphis had taken place. The tenent had become addicted to LSD. Suddenly the windows to the apartment took on purple, blue, green and psychedelic colors as water colors were used to give the stained glass appearance. Much art work was being displayed. The burning aroma of incense and faint smoke from the here to fore religious connotation fumigated the neighborhood. At night weird lights flickered and people walking by the place in white shirts became radioactive and strange eerie irridense showed that something was unusual going on. The volume of traffic increased, laughter and shouts of boys and girls kept the neighbors awake. No one in the surrounding area slept much, loud music blasted from some large hi-ft speaker woofer/tweeter combination and the entire building shook on its foundation. The only time the place was calm was at about high noon when they had either gone into a stupor or the drugs had knocked them out completely. I had never seen a hippy before, I had read a few isolated articles in the paper about places like Greenwhich village, Rittenhouse square in Philadelphia and seen a few pictures of some long haired creeps from San Franciso that started the movement. But here in a quiet peaceful little city who would have imagined that this college graduate would have suddenly started a revolution in the worst way and especially in a nice apartment that I had recently redecorated. It took me about three days to decide to throw the tenent out which after only one day his fears were short lived, one of the culprits had broke into a service station and robbed the cigarette machine, putting the loot in a mail mans pouch he drug it through the snow. The police followed the trail of the sack dragging on the ground and quickly arrested the hippies. So it was crowbar hotel for the first batch of riotous hippies that I had been in contact with. The strangest things also happened with their automobiles. The hoods were taken off, a lot of chrome plated caps and accessories were placed under the hood, stripes and psychedelic paint was used to give the most unusual appearance to the stripped down automobiles, they always made too much noise, and no one ever slept, night and day they gunned the motors and shouted at the top of their voices. They wore the ugliest clothing imaginable, some of them had Army, Navy, Marine Corps and military clothing from all the services, this they chopped up into hideous garments, and no one ever used the shower. The water bill was very nominal during the hippy craze era. But they consumed lots of electricity as there were many lights that revolved and many flickered off and on. It was in the middle of November and they didn't buy oil for the furnace, rather they plugged in electric heaters and run up astronomical electric bills, the fuses would pop about every hour.

When I went to access the damage after the police had cleared the gang out, I couldn't believe my eyes. Everywhere there was psychedelic paint, luminous paints, and radioactive paints. There were vulgar words on the wall, during moments of going under the influence of the LSD: some had unusual artistic talents, there as one wall that had been decorated with paintings of green leaves, thousands of little leaves like oak leaves. Hundreds of hours must have been expended while in some hypnotic trance or delirium tremens to paint these intricate designs. What a waste of effort. The bedroom was one of absolute horror. On the east wall was every obscene word in the hippy vocabulary and all done with radioactive paint so they would glow in the dark. There was one ghost painted on the south wall urinating. What a conglomeration.

I blinked my eyes in utter dismay and then took a look at the living room. The carpet had been ripped off the floor and each floor board of the hard wood flooring painted, the beautiful varnished oak flooring was now one plank green and the next black. What a mess! The icebox was full of rotten food and the strong stench of vinegar erupted when ever the door was opened. I wondered what vinegar was used for in hippy land. Anyhow, it was going to be a task to clean and restore the apartment. Rather than paint the one door that was so scungy with psychedelic colors, perhaps I could use a spare door I had stored in the basement. After nearly working a month in my spare time and on weekends with the help of anyone I could recruit, of course the trouble with recruits they took so long looking at the place he couldn't get much work out of them, it was finally finished. I thought perhaps I could charge 50 cents admission to look at the place and recoup some of my losses. But the task on hand took a complete renovation and redecoration, the furniture was hauled to the dump since the upholstery was full of cigarette or marauana burn holes, and smelled of drugs and smoke. The bathroom was unmentionable, they were flushing the toilet by lifting the plunger manually. Every unmentionable had been jammed into the toilet. It took a large roto rooter to clear the main sewer pipe and a smaller flexible rooter auger to clear the kitchen and bathroom sinks. These people had really done a job on the place. Wax was everywhere. Remnants of large candles stuck in bottles and paraffin wax dripping down the sides in colors were strewn about. The mail bag that had ripped off the postman lay in the middle of the floor. The only thing left on the bed was one mattress and it was laying on the living room floor. What happened to the box springs and frame is still a mystery.

After completing the overhaul of my choice apartment, redecorating it and putting beautiful pastel colors on the walls, trimming all the woodwork and putting new furniture in, with a new wall to wall carpet, I advertised the apartment. A nice elderly lady fell in love with the cute apartment and put down the rent quickly. The experience was over so I thought and everything was completely reconditioned. No more headaches would ensue, the dirty work of the hippies was covered up by the new paint job and it was a bygone era of misfortune and large expenses.

The night the apartment was rented, I received an urgent call from the lady that rented the apartment. She said when she went to bed and turned out the lights that the entire wall lit up with profane words! It didn't make sense, I had painted the wall with super latex paint and nothing was readable on the wall afterwards. However I put on my coat and drove 20 miles to investigate. Sure enough when the lights were extinguished, somehow the light going through the paint caused it to shine through the new paint and make all the nasty words readable. Even that damn urinating ghost showed through the paint. I agreed to repaint the wall that weekend, and I applied two more coats of paint over the last two.

The repaint job did not work at all. The same thing happened. I bought some radioactive paint and changed the spelling of the words to make them read a little pleasant, and repainted the wall for the third time. As an engineer this appeared the most logical way to solve the problem. Then I remembered that lead paint would stop the radiation and I set about trying to find lead paint. That was one of the greatest wild goose chases I had been on. I looked hi and lo for lead paint, the stuff the Navy quite using in favor of zinc chromate. At last I used some primer paint and it apparently had enough metallic substances in it to shield the radiation, the only thing wrong was it had to be repainted twice with the primer and twice more with flat latex. This was eight coats of paint I had put on in less than two weeks. By now I had some nice words to call the hippies but I saved them in case something more terrible came along and it did. A year later the go-go girls were invented. You know the ones that danced in the cages and wore the miniskirts and were usually high on drugs. Lucky I did not get them in the same apartment but what they did to my mobile home I rented to them was something else. If I had been a marathon runner then I would have taken off and never came back!

It was exceedingly dark when a ravishing blond girl knocked, rather tapped on the park office door and a girl like the ones you find in the hurley girly magazines asked if I had any trailers to rent, "yes number 3, the wolverine, is vacant I said" and wrote out a rent receipt and collected the $95.00 which covered the mortgage but not much more. Suzie moved in two more girls with her. They were from Greenwitch village in New York City. Upon obtaining access to the key she ran out in the black of night and all three girls yelled at the top of their voices "Yeh-hooooo!" I just blinked my eyes and wondered what kind of pickle I had associated myself with. At this phase of my life when there were 23 mortgage payments due each month and I was paying financial roulette? There were mortgages on the trailer park, mortgages on every mobile home I owned, my house in Philadelphia, the one the city was giving me a bad time about, and my six apartment houses. Everything had a mortgage on it. Every month I had to spend over three hours just writing out checks. And after doing so I had to eat. It got so bad that someone that held a mortgage didn't get paid that month. I explained to the mortgagors that I was doing my best and my plan was to put all their names in a hat and pull out the one name that was the unlucky one for the month and they had to wait until the next month to get paid. With 23 to 1 odds they got along ok until one time when one didn't get paid for two months but I explained they had made $10 in late charges. It was one of the ultimate cases of high finance but all in all I had established a good credit reference and built up a giant equity at the same time. It took exceptional discipline and courage. It was a period of time I had to depend on a lot of prayers and hope and above all, absolute positive thinking, one negative thought at that time would have spelled disaster. But I was too busy in most cases to realize that the financial burden was really as great as it was. There were always headaches and as mentioned about, the blond was now to become the biggest headache with the exception to the colonel's wife, I had ever known.

Within an hour after renting the mobile home to the vivacious blond go-go girl, my troubles started. Three phone calls came in in rapid succession. Mrs. Brown said she thought the trailer was exploding, that loud noises were buckling the walls and the other lady reported that the concrete blocks supporting the mobile home were crumbling, and my vocabulary was now increased by a new word which I had to look up in the dictionary, which was called quad. I was a sound engineer myself and had designed some elaborate sound systems out in Hollywood. I had even built a thin man coffin which was walling up floor joists and driving them with a large 15 inch speaker, but nothing could compare with this quad. It consisted of four giant speakers driven by high power two channel amplifiers. My cat crawled into the speaker enclosure, but went berserk and disappeared for a week.

Even my folded 16 foot klipsch horn was no match for the sound that came from the trailer. To make matters worse cars came in volley up the hill. You would think they were holding a rock festival, such a long haired bunch I had never seen before since my experience with the hippies that had vandalized my Malibu estates, so as I called the upper lower middle class apartments. The noise stopped suddenly and they all piled into automobiles giggling and shaking their anatomy, but I had not seen anything yet. Anyway, they were leaving and peace and quiet was restored, that was until about

3:30 a.m. When suddenly I was awaken to the sound of thunder being played at 33 ½ rpms, all the lights were on in the trailer park, the twenty six tenants peered out their windows standing sleepy-eyed and nerve shaken, supporting themselves by hanging onto the drapes. But they came fully awake instantaneously because the three go-go girls were dancing to the Beetles in their work costumes which were very scant, and they had on the tall boots and were topless. Someone drew the white curtains in the girl's trailer and numerous tenants in the park could only see the silhouettes of the dancers which was still entertaining except to their wives. They started calling the landlord and voicing complaints. At this point I would have gladly refunded twice their money back plus double their security deposit. After about an hour the orgy died out and everything was back to normal. This was a new situation. I had never heard of a go-go girl and did not quite know what course of action to take but I realized that they had to go that was for sure. I quickly headed to my lawyer and made out a petition with precepts which was a fancy word for eviction notice, but the lawyer said it would take a while to get them out.

The second night was worse than the first: the male tenants in the park did not go to sleep but stayed up watching the late, late show until the real show took place at about 3:00 a.m. Things got so bad that I went deep into my creative mind to figure out an antidote to the racket. There must have been seven cars in front of the 50 foot trailer, the three go-goers were really going strong and the wives started calling and complaining. Mainly because their husbands were watching through the shades and some had purchased new binoculars for the occasion. I had to put a stop to the racket, no city police were available, the county didn't ever want to get involved but they were really disturbing the peace. So I went straight to the main circuit breaker box that controlled the power to the trailer, the primary power, the 220 volts alternating current. The big grey box with the huge circuit breaker the 200 ampere jobbie, with one quick yank I flipped off the power and heard sounds like screams, what the hell! What's going on! Damn! I went to the rear door of the trailer and opened it and yelled at the top of my voice "it's a raid" and that statement really got action fast, guys started beating it, some got in their cars and went flying down the hill. All I could see was a steady stream of tail lights going down the hill. When I returned to my office the phone was ringing, only this time it was from the husbands, they said the lights were off in No.3 and to check it out. I said "ok" but went to bed instead. It was the first chance I had to sleep in over two hours. After about half an hour I heard a feeble knock on the door and the blond go-go dancer said she had an electrical problem. "Did you pay your bill?" I asked her. The electric company shut it off perhaps? She left and mumbled "at this hour of the night?" Yeh, they are clamping down on the delinquent accounts. We'll check on it tomorrow, I'll call the electrician and see what he can find. Everyone got a good sleep that night and my creative mind and engineering talent had paid off again. Now if only they would serve the eviction papers and start the legal proceedings to oust the trio and their followers. I realized that the only thing I was responsible for was "quiet enjoyment" but there was nothing quiet about those dancers, they didn't even know what the word quiet meant. I thought of other drastic measures to take to try to make life as miserable for them as they were for the whole park, but gave up on the mental canivery and decided to just shut off the water. This was one of the biggest mistakes I made, because without water the toilet wouldn't flush, but they kept right on using it and without water they couldn't clean up all the spilled drinks, the dishes the places started to smell raunchy. It was at that point necessary to turn the water back on. But now the junk in the toilet plugged up over 500 feet of secondary underground sewer pipes, they were so blocked that even the roto rooter wouldn't do any good. I had to literally dig up the pipes and replace some of them. It was back to the ole shovel again for me. I would have ran that day if only I had know about running, it would have been nice to run, to escape. Near the end of the year 1982 I sold the resort park and left it with the only two manufactured homes, one for my daughter and one for Betty and himself.

My wife and I moved back into our original home at Tuxedo Park for two years where I continued to run ultra marathons, marathons and all kinds of shorter races until my heart attack. In 1984 we moved into our five family apartments on Bell road. I had my heart attack in May 1983 and retired on January 2nd 1986. In September 1983 I started art lessons and continued them until the year 2001. It 1989 we sold our five family apartment and bungalow and moved to our present location in Rome, NY

CHAPTER 20

JOHN R. HUCKABY ART CAREER

I inherited the gift of art from my father who could draw most anything and paint them. This natural ability was perhaps my greatest assets.

From the time when I entered kindergarten I could draw and paint. The teachers were amazed at my ability to sketch animals and people. This gift from God remained with me all through my life into old age.

To supplement my gift from God, I spent four years attending night classes at the Long Beach, California Academy of Art between World War 2 and the start of the Korean conflict, when he was called to active duty in the Navy reserve. I was fortunate to have finished art school before being sent overseas.

Upon the end of the Korean conflict I resumed classes for a short time until I took a job as soul radio operator and technician on a Greek tramp steamer when the radio operator deserted and they needed someone to take the SS Anthony form San Pedro to Walvas Bay, South Africa. This was an opporture chance for me to see the world and sketch the interesting scenes all over the world that I had not seen during my war years. I had already learned to speak Japanese and now was the only one aboard ship except one sailor that could speak English. I learned the Greek language quickly as being the soul radio operator with his high speed dit dahs. The most important thing was my opportunity to see the world and visit the famous art galleries in Germany, France, Amsterdam, England and many throughout the world in over a half dozens of trips around the world.

My three year job in France and England also gave me insight on the work's of the old masters. Also my trips to Greece, Turkey, Saudi Arabia and Israel were good background studies along the many trips around Africa proved helpful. I spent some time in Goa and Mormogao, India, Saigon, Indo China and Japan.

All of my extensive world travels gave me inspiration something deep inside that wanted to come out and the best way was with art. Not abstract but what I saw and felt. How lucky I was to have learned Gods formula of how to put all these things on paper and canvas. From my studies in dynamic symmetry I had the key the secret of God's design. You can't tell me there was not a Creator and He was not super intelligent. Yes there is a Designer, Creator with a purpose and a purpose to our life and to our universe.

I have painted most of the book of Genesis and Revelation from the bible along with many other related truthful and practical instructions to live by and yet have found no reason to sincerely doubt any of God's word or promise.

My heart attack came on May 15, 1983 at Ottawa, Canada during the last few yards of a standard 26.2 mile marathon. This resulted in a loss of one of my coronary arteries and over a third of my heart muscle turned to scar tissue, this resulted in curtailing my running career. It was time for me to use my artistic ability that I had possessed since childhood and I had practiced since and completed four years of study at the Long Beach Academy of Art at Long Beach California from June 1946 to June 1950. Between the end of his US Navy tour of duty and the start of the Korean Conflict in June 1950.

I had realized it had been 33 years since my formal schooling in art and painting. To catch up on the new art forms and drawing techniques it would be profitable to take lessons locally at the Rome art and community center. So I started classes in the September of 1983 and continued for the next 17 years. My first instructor was Mr. Roger Morris who taught me to just use the pencil and draw still life and models. He progressed and in the second semester paint with the brush and oil paints. I was on my way. I painted with the God given gift and talent. I won a host of blue ribbons and painted many top award winning paintings, "A tribute to Bishop Asbury" was judged best of show in the 30th annual spring show of the Rome art association in the Rome art and community center on April 18, 1988. My art instructor at the time was the most memorable person, Mrs. Penny Simons who later met with the most unfortunate accident. She died from an overdose of some medicine, due to a hospital error.

Another great teacher was Jane Taylor. She taught me how to paint murals. It was easy for me because of my work as an engineer. It had taught me to scale things and it made the task much simpler. She was responsible for my venture into painting murals. The murals that I have painted nationwide and for foreign countries are shown in this book. One of the foremost teachers that I was truly fortunate to have had as an art instructor was Matthew LoRusso. He was a professional artist with over thirty years with the New York Department of Transportation. Matt was so dedicated to painting he could be found in sub freezing temperatures wearing battery heated gloves. Matt was a great teacher. He could help the students in all types of mediums. Matt died doing what he loved most. Teaching, painting and drawing beautiful landscapes and portraits. At the death of Matt, the teaching position was given to me, who taught at the Ava Dorfman senior citizen center at Rome NY. I continued teaching for ten years until retiring in the year 2008. I love the volunteer work and enjoyed seeing my students win awards. Proof that the seniors still have so much to give to the world in their latter years.

Perhaps the word zeal most describes the way I attacked the profound state of self actualization which flowered and tenaciously drove me into a desire to get up off the floor and use my last God given gift to rise above the mundane day to day retirement with nearly half my heart missing and not being able to even slow jog.

In retrospect I clearly remember the first day in art class at the Rome art community center at Rome, NY in September 1983. Our art instructor was Mr. Roger Morris, a graduate from Chanard art school at Los Angeles, Ca and had a large background in many art forms. He had perfected a unique art form of textured glazes using pearl hues in variegated iridescent layers. They were very pretty and had commercial appeal. The first day he set up a display for us to draw; oatmeal can, a pair of scissors and an eraser.

It was fun to get back in the drawing and painting. Roger took us students through our lessons and we practiced for several years drawing and painting most everything from nudes to still life. I was dedicated to the art and won a lot of awards and ribbons in those early days.

However I did not reach my true God given talent until three years later in 1986 when approached by the pastor of the first united Methodist church at Rome NY.

The Rev. Richard McCaughey contacted me to paint a framed mural. It was titled "the sower." Four other artists joined with me to produce the mural, Mr. Frank Ray Sr,. Claudia Gassner Hartz, Diane Brockway and Dennis Dixon. I had visited the Sea of Galilee when working in Saudi Arabia in 1977, and had a good mental description of its location and surroundings. From that picture I was able to prepare a working sketch.

The mural was painted in the educational building of the church, it was large, eight feet high and sixteen feet wide. It depicted Jesus first parable in which he told how the word of God would be received by and acted upon by the people. The theme is generally the Galilean ministry of Christ and included a 50 mile wide area around the Sea of Galilee covering the full scope from Nazareth to Caesarea Phillippi at Mount Hermon.

I projected my sketch on the canvas which had been double gessoed to preserve it for hundreds of years. The mural was framed in basswood from a tree in Lee Center, NY. I researched and organized the project and described the history of the mural. The mural was dedicated in a ribbon cutting ceremony at 11 a.m. Sunday, November 23, 1986. The beginning of John's prolific mural output locally and afar.

JOHN HUCKABY AND CREW UNVIEL MURAL

Upon completion of the mural, my friend, Frank Ray a copainter of the mural pointed at the eight foot by sixteen foot painting in a hall of the First Methodist church at 212 W. Embargo St., in Rome, NY and spoke. "John you had come back to do the mural" Ray said.

The mural, centered on the theme of "The Sower," portrays Jesus teaching the multitude from a boat on the sea of Galilee. It's dedication included a brief drama and a song about the mural composed and sung by Vicki Cucci.

It took nearly a year from conception to completion. The idea of the mural was conceived by Rev. Richard McCaughey. I directed the painting with Mr. Frank Ray as my assistant along with Claudia Gassner Hartz of Utica, an art teacher at St. Paul elementary school in Whitesboro, Diane Brockway and Dennis Dixon a sergeant.

In 1974, I was not a painter but a communication electronics engineer at Griffith air force base at Rome, NY. I had begun running to strengthen my heart, and completed over a hundred ten marathons and a dozen ultra marathons. Some over a hundred miles long plus the grueling Hawaiian triathalon.

But the coronary attack in May 1983 put a stop to all that. And when I was in the hospital, I looked out the window and saw the beautiful scenery and wanted to paint it. That wish came true when I returned to Lee Center, NY my home and took courses at the Rome art and community center. It was about that time that I bumped into Frank Ray Sr. near age seventy at an art festival. He was the former owner of Ray's drive in and an accomplished artist. He could sculpt as well as paint and he was first vice president of the Rome art association and I later became second vice president. When the project began I was 67 years old and was asked to do some initial sketches and I eventually became principal artist, director and researcher. The mural started off as a rather simple concept, but it grew into a complex piece of art McCaughey said.

JOHN R. HUCKABY'S ART CAREER

After a few months of research, I made a color pencil sketch on 8 inch by 20 inch paper. A second working drawing was enlarged to about five times that size.

The frame stretcher for the canvas as well as the outside frame was hand made by McCaughey, whose hobby was carpentry. Because of the length of the wood, a tree had to be specially cut at a sawmill.

The mural was so large that at first there was no place to buy canvas. Finally, we purchased a triangular piece of sail canvas. It took four men to stretch it on the frame.

Then the artist took over. Ray and I worked mostly everyday and we were joined by Claudia Gassner Hartz of Utica, Sgt. Dennis Dixon and Dianne Brockway.

The painting contains 60 human characters, many of them bearing similarities to church members and 59 animals and birds.

The scene is a scaled down portion of northern Israel, including the villages of Tiberius, Hayman, Genesaret, Magdala, Tabgah and Capernuam as well as Mount Tabor (site of the transfiguration) and Mount Hermon.

To achieve authentic authenticity many books and documents were checked. I also relied on my memories of the area, I spent vacation time there when working in the middle east as an engineer.

The mural is still on display, years since it was dedicated on Sunday, November 23, 1986. Several thousand postcards were made of the mural and some are still available.

With the advent of my work on "The Sower" mural for the first united Methodist church at Rome, NY., I began an unbelievable painting spree. I painted a portrait of my mother in law, Henrietta Bonnet Gillespie. She was born in Chatellrault, France on December 8, 1886, a countess and sole heir to the family rich grape vineyards near Bordeux, France. She had a profound love for animals. During WWI she went to Paris and met her husband who took her for a ride in his motorcycle side car. Next day he left for the front lines and was gassed and sent to Arizona for two years. He returned and married her, she returned to America with my wife Betty. She died at age 99 years and six months. Her portrait is in a collection of her daughter's. Copies of the painting size 3 ½' x 2' can be found in nursing homes as they contain painting of her cat and dog Suzzette. The painting along with one of my wife at age four named "Sassy Betty" was received several awards. Henrietta was painted in 1985.

Henrietta

The year 1987 found me painting a mural of the Boonville Fair which is located at the fair's museum today. It was an amazingly complex work of art which shows most of the events of the fair. The framed mural was 5'x4' and was painted while the fair was in progress, with spectators watching. I also painted the over 100 musicians of a drum and bugle band. Also the carnival, demolition derby, grandstand, jumping horses and the entire fairground. In addition I painted the portrait of the fair's executive director.

It was the year 1988 I became fully overpowered with the religious past of the city of Rome, NY. Once again the first united Methodist church gave me an assignment to paint the historical visits of the greatest preacher to this region Bishop Francis Asbury. After doing research I was overwhelmed with awe at what he did for the early settlers of this area. It was in the year 1799 that bishop Asbury, a circuit rider preacher would visit here then called Fort Stanwix. Bishop Asbury in his lifetime rode horse back for over forty four years; his home was his saddle and his parish the continent. He rode close to three quarter million miles horseback covering the region and died at Spotsilvania from pneumonia. He met at the home, a cabin, of Jonathan Newman, leader of the Methodist society. This was the inspiration needed for my greatest painting.

I spent several weeks researching all available information and visiting the local Fort Stanwix historical site here at Rome, NY to obtain authentic details of that period. This proved advantageous, as my painting could be an exact replica of the original and produce strong eye appeal.

I had a lot going for myself in addition to researching the history of the memorable event. The drafting courses I had taken at the Long Beach City College and used in my daily job as an engineer was a plus as I had to portray the inside of a cabin with people the outside through windows and door. The people inside were in addition to Bishop Asbury some of the most important as time passed, the young child portrait Benjamin Wright who along with Jervis engineered the Erie canal construction. Included were Jonathan Newman, leader of the Methodist society and Joshua Hathaway that became first postmaster and turned over first shovel of dirt to start building the Erie Canal July 4, 1817.

On April 18 1988 my painting titled "a tribute to Bishop Asbury" was judged best of show in the 30th annual spring show of the Rome art and community center. More than 125 works were judged and placed on display.

On October 8, 1987 I painted in the barn festival of the arts and received a first place award for my painting in oils that was titled, "Malinowski Farm" I, John Huckaby of Rome, second vice president of the Rome art association also received the Norstar bank award, a ribbon and $50 savings bond for my oil painting exhibited in the 1987 art show.

The painting titled "Malinowski Farm" also won first place in the oils category in recent Rome art association regional fine arts exhibit.

Malinowski Farm
Best of show

My decision to paint "Malinowski Farm" and the inspiration to make it a winner was due to Mr. Malinowski who owned and operated the large farm on Sterns Rd in Lee Center, NY whose son did parachute jumps for charity. The son took pictures of the farm while descending in his parachute. I took the photos and used them to depict an air view of the farm. The results were astounding! My painting had a unique perspective that made it a winner in many art shows. Unfortunate for Mr Malinowski and his son, his son was killed in 1986 when his parachute failed to open. I gave the painting to Mr. Malinowski who prized it in memory of his dear son.

Again in 1988 I was asked to paint the history of the local first united Methodist church at Rome. My research found the history to be very fascinating. I had already painted the best of show "A tribute to Bishop Asbury" and decided on three additional paintings to portray the church beginnings from 1799 onward.

The first painting shows Bishop Francis Asbury, riding from Philadelphia on a circuit to tend flocks of worshipers in the northeast. He traveled over 275,000 miles in his 44 year ministry The second painting focuses on spiritual growth in the community as the small society sets up for Sunday services in an old school house down town Rome, then Fort Stanwix in 1802.

My third painting of the church history was called "Fellowship" it portrait the congregation's first church building at the foot of church street. It was dedicated January 1, 1829. It was the first Methodist church in America built with a steeple.

The last painting, titled "missions" is a mini mural of the life of Dr. Welthy Honsinger Fisher and flanked on two sides by portraits of the world famed humanitarian one at age 28 and another when she was nearing 80 years of age.

She was the founder of literacy village in Lucknow, India. She graduated from RFA and Syracuse University, a native of Rome, NY. She was married to a Methodist bishop of India and Burma. Dr. Fisher also served as a Methodist missionary in China. She founded world education inc. and president from 1959 to 1972. She traveled, lectured and wrote, doing everything she could to teach the world to read and write. I had little difficulty in finding needed inspiration to paint the four dear historic paintings for the first united Methodist church home of Dr. Wealthy Honsinger Fisher, she died at age 101 on December 16, 1980. The great leader of India Mah Atma Ghandi once said, "She left I saw God's footprints all over the floor."

I painted two other murals for the church. One was titled "The cry of the poor" an oil 6'x5' which portrayed Christ helping the hungry. I painted the local Methodist church with the needy people in line waiting to enter the church to obtain the food donated by the local grocery stores. It was perhaps my most sincere effort to paint the goodness of the church, however my efforts were far too good in the fact the people I portrayed in the long line were too exacting and they most all recognized themselves in the "bread line" this resulted in an onrush of complaints and the mural was quickly stored in the church cellar.

The last painting I did for the Methodist church was the huge framed mural 9'x18' which portrayed the entire last book of the bible "Revelation." It encompassed the world today and its joyful or gloomy future; which ever the apostle John described our faith in Jesus Christ would determine the outcome of our lives. I painted it exactly as described with the one small exception, placing a flag at the 18th hole a symbol of God's provision. It took me over a year to sketch and paint the large mural but I gained a lot of hope from my endeavors.

"Best of Show"

DOCTER WEALTHY FISHER
METHODIST MISSIONARY
SIZE: 2' X 4' OIL
LOCATED: FIRST UNITED
METHODIST CHURCH, ROME, NY.

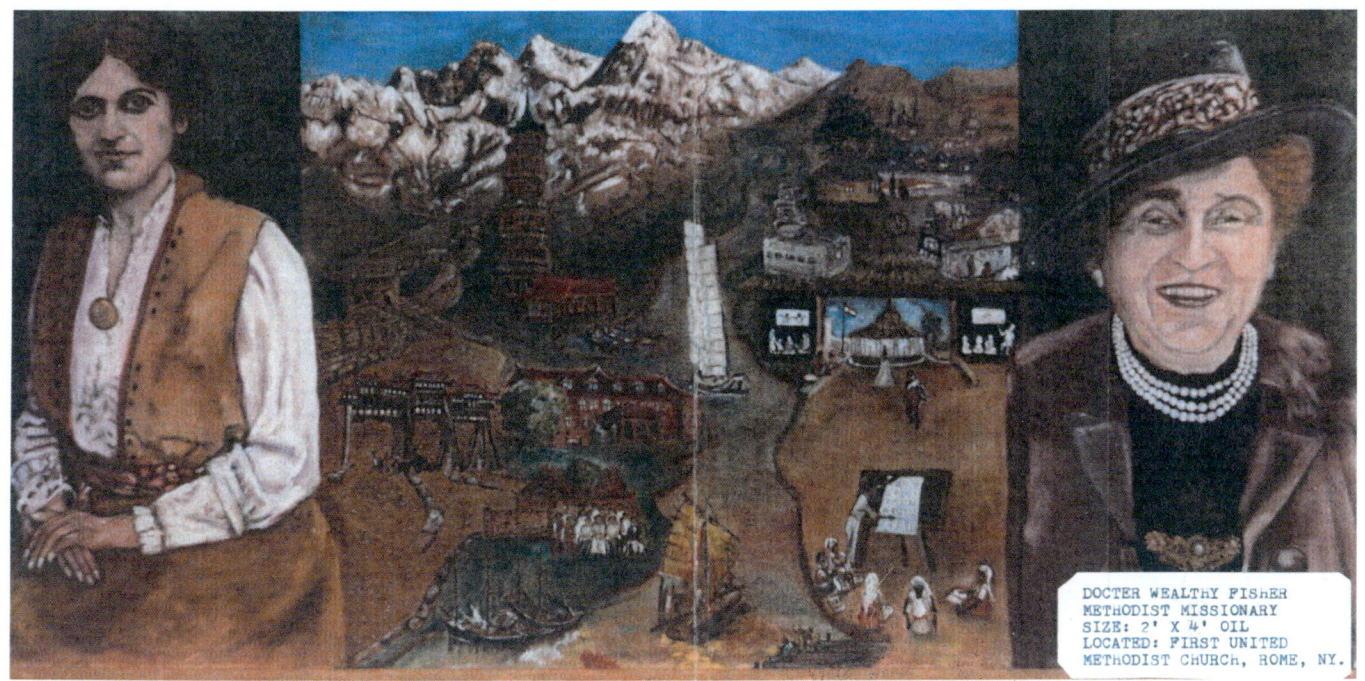

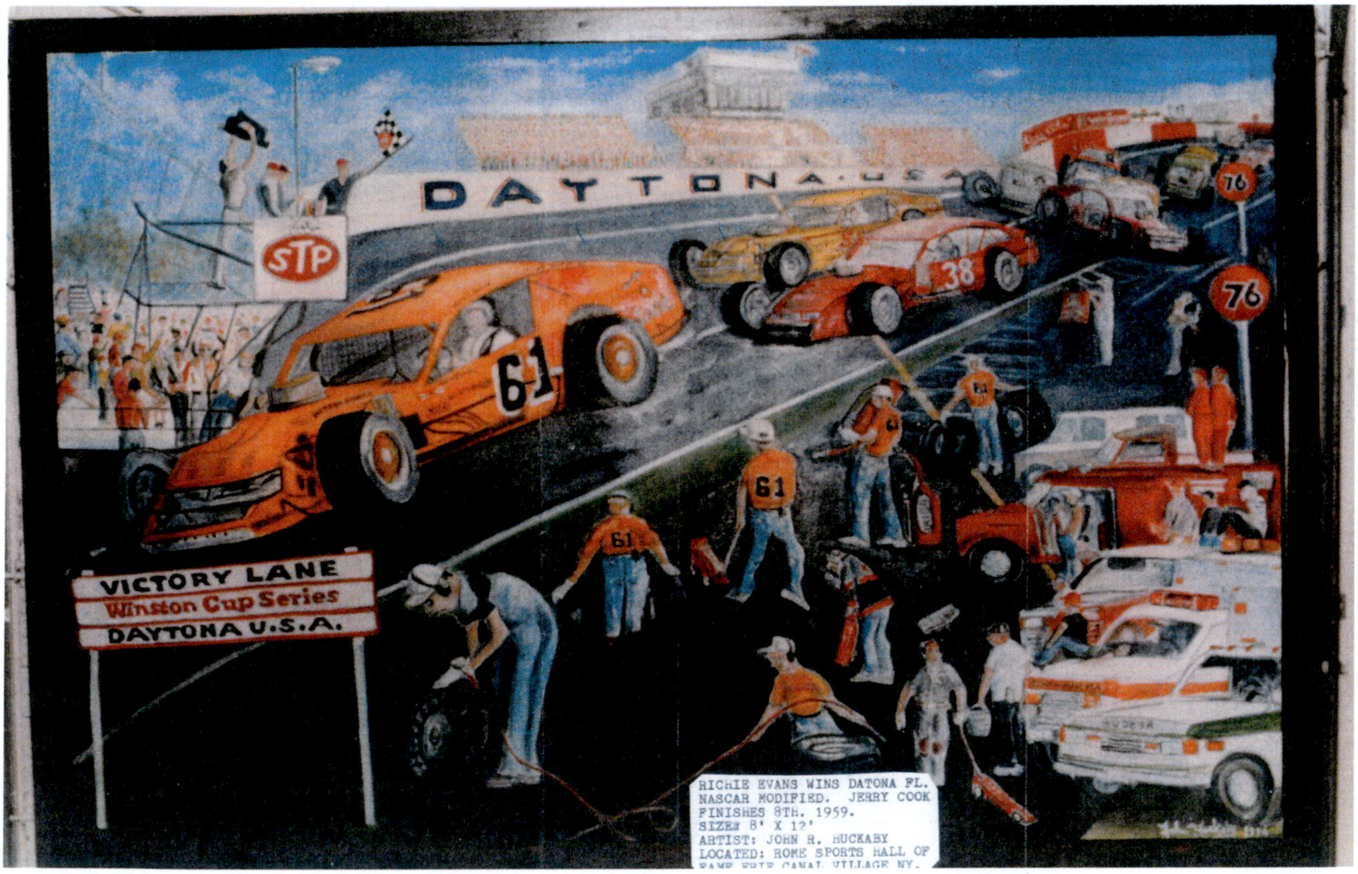
DAYTONA U.S.A
STP
76
38
61
VICTORY LANE
Winston Cup Series
DAYTONA U.S.A.
RICHIE EVANS WINS DATONA FL.
NASCAR MODIFIED. JERRY COOK
FINISHES 8TH. 1959.
SIZE: 8' X 12'
ARTIST: JOHN R. HUCKABY
LOCATED: ROME SPORTS HALL OF
FAME ERIE CANAL VILLAGE NY.

THE BOOK OF REVELATION MURAL
SIZE: 10' X 19' OIL
ARTIST: JOHN R. HUCKABY
LOCATED: FIRST UNITED METHO-
DIST CHURCH, ROME, NY.

DAVE PACKER SET SPEED BOAT
RECORD AT HONOLULU 1959 MUR.
SIZE: 8' X 15' OIL
ARTIST: JOHN R. HUCKABY
LOCATED: ROME SPORTS HALL OF
FAME AT ERIE CANAL VILLAGE
ROME, NY.

It was on the 4th of July, Independence Day 1990 I stretched an 8 foot by 15 foot long canvas and started painting a mural of Dave Packer setting a world power boat record off the coast of Honolulu, Hawaii in 1979.

The mural was painted by me for the Rome Sports Hall of Fame Museum located at the Erie Canal village Rome, NY.

The mural depicted a background of Pearl Harbor to Diamond Head, with the Koulau mountains, Aloha tower, Mona Alamona and Waikki beaches.

It took me three months to paint the mural, in my daughter's garage. She and her children were in the back yard celebrating the 4th and America was involved in the Gulf war at the oil fields with Iraq and Sadam Hussain.

The mural was filled with great detail and I was fully knowledgeable of the area and painted it with a high degree of authenticity. I depicted the power boat race just as it was held, with Mr. Dave Packer setting the world power boat record. Words cannot begin to describe the action filled mural

Now in the year 2010, twenty years later, the mural is suspended over the museum doorway is a tourist attraction. I had my first art instructor to critique the painting and advise me on the final work of art prior to it being dedicated and insured, Mr. Roger Morris made several trips and offered suggestions and color details in the mural. I served on the museum board of directors under Miss Ruth Demere, executive director of the Rome sports hall of fame.

During the year of 1994, I painted my mini mural of Tony Washington in the world Olympics held at Barcelona, Spain in 1992. The mural depicted Tony Washington a Blackman Discus thrower competing in his event. The back ground of the mural was highly descriptive and accurate. It showed the entire event and all the background panorama of the stadium and interesting parts of the city. A snicker wrapper floating to the ground represented his sponsor.

The last mural was dedicated on November 2, 1996. It was a framed mural 6' by 7' and hung from the large entrance door at the end of the museum.

The mural was a tribute to and honors memory of Richie Evans and salutes Jerry Cook, modified racing champions who both have been enshrined in the Rome sports hall of fame. I researched over 400 of Richie's races before I settled on the one I used for inspiration for the mural. The 1980 Daytona modified nascar which Richie won and Jerry Cook finished 8th. I took great care to recreate the finish and included members of his crew and family. Richie was killed at age 43 in a practice run accident at Marinsville speedway in 1985. Evans was inducted into NASCAR Hall of Fame Jan 2012.

During the late summer of 1996 two nice ladies from the Westmoreland Methodist church contacted me to paint a mural for their church in Westmoreland, NY. They agreed to pay for the materials and I agreed to paint the mural labor free. We agreed upon the subject matter and chose to show Jesus loving and curing the poor, lame and neglected children as well as those who had better lives and more fortunate. The title "Jesus and the Children."

I didn't have much to go on and just went with my idea of how things were and what the dress and style of children and Jesus was at that time in history.

It took me three months to sketch and paint the mural size 6'x9'. I remember painting a rich child offering Jesus four beautiful roses for her blessing and another poor child with only a blade of grass, another with a cane and a rabbit behind a stone. The scene was perfect and they gave me $700.00 for all the materials and delivery.

JESUS AND THE CHILDREN
SIZE: 6' x 9' OIL
ARTIST: JOHN R. HUCKABY
LOCATED: UNITED METHODIST
CHURCH WESTMORLAND, NY

JESUS PRAYING OVER THE SINS OF THE WORLD.
SIZE: 3' X 4'
ARTIST: JOHN R. HUCKABY
LOCATION: SEVENTH DAY ADVENTIST
CHURCH, ROME NY

The painting was dedicated during church services ceremony at the Westmoreland United Methodist church November 3, 1996 by guest pastor Madeline McDonald. The two ladies responsible for the mural were and commissioned it were Mrs. Judy Bachman and Mrs. Pat Johnson, who were active in the restoration of the old church.

A large amount of scriptural data was incorporated in the mural relating to Christ's concern for children. I worked during the late summer in my garage to paint the mural with little distractions.

In the fall of 1998 I attended a series of lectures given at the seventh day Adventists church on the bible book of Daniel. The pastor Rev. Rick Juntz had me paint a mini mural framed to be hung above the alter in the sanctuary. I choose the title and description of "Jesus praying over the sins of the world." The mural depicted Jesus with his body laying over the world hands clasped in prayer.

The next painting for the church came as unexpected meeting with a medical missionary with the seventh day Adventist church Robert Pannekoek on his way from Australia to a teaching job in Virginia. He took all of John's paintings with him to use as illustrations in telling the story of Daniel and his dreams as described in the bible. I painted five scenes from the bible, the metallic man, a winged lion, a bear with three ribs in his mouth, a four headed leopard and a dragon. The metallic man was about 7 foot tall, I ripped 2x4's to make the frames and sized the canvas with Gesso, to embalm the paintings.

It was so hot painting in the garage I went out under a tree by the road; this caused a traffic jam by the curiosity seekers. One fellow wanted me to paint a black leopard on his living room wall. Before looking for a paint brush I read the whole story from the bible. Daniel's predictions have come true.

Four days prior to Christmas 1996 to 1998 Saint John the Baptist Cathonic church at Rome, NY contacted me to paint four stage show drops. The first being a country scene with sheep grazing and the star of Bethlehem overhead. The next painting was the interior of Mary's home with a credenza (urn) by the door. The third painting was the birth of Jesus location and the fourth theater drop was the interior of the court where Pilate had Jesus judged. These drops were 6'x8' in size and I was able to get them done for the show by painting into the wee hours of the morning. I used Japan Dryer so they would quickly dry. The birth of Jesus stage show was very successful and a real baby was used.

I painted during the period of 1995 to 1997 several award winning paintings one of their yearly carnival for their rectory, it has also used to print up over five hundred T-shirts which sold out quickly. I painted several portraits of charismatic interesting older men like the "Old Duffer," "The Chicken Farmer" and one of their elderly Priest Father Wood. My favorite was Jesus leaving the tomb which I painted for their Easter Mass. I also remember painting a green Christmas tree with 10" holes in it so kids standing behind put their faces in it for decorations.

Another theater drops I painted were for a stage shown taken after the movie "Greece" the first drop was an Italian house frontage in the early 1900's and the other into today's modern era. The play was a musical with songs so descriptive. The stage show was held at Procter high school at Utica, NY. At half time the curtain of the old house was removed and the modern one put up. I filmed the show and the next day evening went to the Utica Masonic Lodge graduation ceremony where I received my diploma of graduation and becoming a 32 degree mason.

One morning while having breakfast with the boy's one fellow asked me to paint a mural of the Masonic history. I joined the masons to learn their history and what a painting would show.

The history of the Masonic order was most inspirational. I painted the history from Adam and Eve to our present existence. The most important thing was the strict training of teaching in the way we live and conduct our lives. It was joyful and educational and made much sense on the way we conduct our lives and treat our fellow man. Step by step in my mural I traced the wonderful history and the common sense that lay therein. The mural was about 7'x8' and framed then installed in the lodge at the lodge in Rome, NY. Later the building was sold and the mural is presently installed in the Masonic lodge at Lee Center, NY.

I honestly believe that if young boys becoming men world over could learn the common sense of how to live among each other the world would be a paradise.

I went on to become a historian in the Amaranth and Eastern star orders of the masons. And painted the "Amaranth" mural 8'x12' wide. In 1999 the mural depicted Queen Christina of Sweden holding the ritual with local members in the drama. I left the order with my wife and daughter who acted as honorable matron of the Amarants. My health failed and I could no longer join the parades.

One of the most intriguing and educational murals I ever painted was the "History of the Iroquois Indians" which I painted for the local Indian Nation convention center near Oneida, NY. In 2001 while researching their history was very amazed at how they told their existence on this earth and how it all started. Sky woman argues with sky man and falls through a stump hole from heaven and lands on wings of ducks that lower her onto back of a giant sea turtle, sky man follows and they had children, (just like Cain and Abel) who killed and other children fought. One Indian Hiawatha (not Longfellows) had three daughters killed and visualized the Iroquois Nation as a giant eagle in a tree whose roots formed the Indian Nations: Mohawk, Oneida, Onondaga, Cayuga, and Seneca the 6th when the Tuscaroras 125 years later were thrown out of North Carolina. Tadohaho was a deformed ugly chief but agreed when Hiawatha sang to him. The Indian nations today meet yearly and if a man dies his widow takes his place at Syracuse NY. The American government in many ways resembles of the Iroquois Indians. Their spirit worship continued and Christianity is slow to convert. "The history of the Iroquois Indians" mural was painted in the year 2001 and given to Mr. Arthur Pierce who presented it to the conference center. I also painted portraits of famous Indians Redcloud, Sitting Bull and Geronimo. The mini mural was 4'high and 3'wide and framed on canvas.

The mural I painted entitled "Westward Ho" was completed and it was 5' high by 8' wide. The mural showed the early frontier travelers crossing the "great divide" that narrow gap in the Rocky Mountains in Wyoming. It was the only gap for wagons to pass through on their way to California, Montana, Washington or the far west. It was discovered by the Lewis and Clark exposition. The gap was about 20 miles wide. I painted the landscape and the wagon trains crossing a large stream and Indians hunting Buffalo, and put a traveler with a broken push cart in the picture also an Indian Tepee with children and animals to make the painting look the way it was during the start of the gold rush. In 1979 I ran 100 miles from Squaw valley over the High sierra mountains, when at the peak of the mountain Garnet Chief I looked down at Donner's pass and saw the spot where the Donners wagon was caught in the blind pass and they resorted to cannibalism of their dead children to stay alive.

IRIOQUOIS INDIAN HISTORY
SIZE: 5' X 4' OIL
ARTIST: JOHN R. HUCKABY

IRIOQUOIS INDIAN MURAL
KEY

1. SKY MAN AND SKY WOMAN LIVE IN PARADISE. SKY WOMAN GETS ANGRY AND FALLS THROUGH UPROOTED TREE HOLE TO EARTH, DUCKS LOWER HER TO BACK OF GIANT SEA TURTLE WHO TAKES HER ASHORE WHERE SHE STARTS EARTHLY INDIANS WHO ARE MEAN AND FIGHT EACH OTHER.
2. HIAWATHA HAD THREE DAUGHTERS KILLED. INSTEAD OF FIGHTING HE TOOK BEADS AND MADE THE FIRST WAMPUM; SYMBOL OF PEACE.
3. HIAWATHA MET A PROPHET NAMED DEKANAWEDA WHO VISUALIZED AN EAGLE IN THE FORM OF A HUGE TREE. THE ROOTS WERE THE FIVE INDIAN NATIONS. SENECA, ONONDAGA, CAYUGA, ONEIDA AND MOHAWK NATIONS. HIAWATHA AND DEKANAWEDA CONVINCED ALL BUT TADODAHO, ONONDAGA CHIEF, WHO WAS WAR LIKE, MEAN AND HAD GREEN SNAKES IN HIS HAIR. THEY SANG TO HIM AND WON HIM.
4. SACHEMS (SENITORS) MET YEARLY AND THE IROQUOIS NATIONS WERE UNITED AND STRONG. THEY SENT 50 SACHEMS AND IF ONE CHIEF DIED HIS WIFE WOULD ACT IN HIS PLACE. THE AMERICAN GOVERNMENT IS DESIGNED AFTER THEM.
5. PILGRAMS WITH A PRIEST ARE GREETING A TUSCARORA INDIAN THEY RAN THE TUSCARORA INDIANS FROM NORTH CAROLINA AND THEY FLED TO BECOME THE SIXTH IRIQUOIS INDIAN NATION ABOUT YEAR 1715.
6. THE YEARLY COUNCIL WAS HELD NEAR SYRACUSE, N.Y. IT WAS CALLED THE HAUDENOSAUNEE (SIX IRIQUOIS NATIONS CONFEDERACY) ITS CONSTITUTION CALLED KAIANEREKOWA (THE GREAT LAW OF PEACE) IT EXISTS TODAY.
7. THE MEDICINE MAN IS SELF EXPLANATORY, WAR AND DISEASE MADE HIM A MUST. THE IROQUOIS INDIANS LIVED IN THE NORTHEAST IN LONG HOUSES. TWO FAMILIES WOULD SHARE A COMMON FIRE. THEY ALSO BELIEVED IN IMMORTALITY.

My mural Westward-Ho is at the Central Wyoming College, Riverton, Wyoming. The mural was painted in the year 2006 and it took about five months to complete.

In the summer of 2005 I completed painting the Abraham and Crucifixion of Jesus murals The Abraham mural showed him leaving Ur of the Chaldeans with his father Terah both leading the clan. Abraham's wife Sarah riding behind on a donkey and behind her was Hagar her handmaid caring a basket of fruit. Lot, Abraham's cousin was painted tending the sheep. As the bible says, Hagar produced a son named Ishmael and Sara produced Issac.

The Abraham mural was 5' by 6' and the "Crucifixion of Jesus" mural was approximately the same size. These two murals are located at St. Volodymr the Great Ukrainian Catholic church in Utica, NY.

In the year 2005 I completed the painting referred to as the "Veterans Mural." It is 8' by 7' and is framed. the mural showed the three administrations of the department of Veterans Affairs composed of Health, Benefits, and National Cemetary. In my mind it was a symbol of "Peaace on Earth" the mural depicted the many benefits provided to the veterans and the lower half showed scenes from WWII of the land, air and sea battles. The painting was orginally installed in the VA office downtown Rome, NY and later moved with the VA office to the Business and Technology Park Conference Center in Rome, NY.

In the year 2006 I painted the 6' x 8' mural named "The Creation Story and Paradise Lost" mural. It showed the bible description in the book of Genesis of the creation of the earth and everything in it. It illustrated God speaking and the existance of the universe created and day by day through the seven days what the bible stated. My painting was a pictorial description of the creation and the result that came about when Adam and Eve went astray while God was sleeping on His throne in Heaven. The painting followed the sequence of the bibles story and is logical because everything had to come about in correct sequence or life could not exist. Eg. Light, water, land, heat, fish, animals and then mankind (Adam and Eve) would have food, clothing and shelter. It did not take the first humans long to fall victims to the devil and become sinful. Today we are blessed I have Jesus Christ as Savior to trust in.

In the same year I painted a minimural 18" x 24" on June 14. It was titled "Paradise Lost" the mural was a painting of Adam and Eve hiding in the bushes and both dinosaurs and wild animals on this earth are shown together. The idea to paint this unusual painting was due to a discovery of man's footprints and those of dinosaurs found together in an archaeological discovery of stone excavations. Added proof of recent creation and support of creation over evaluation.

The two above apaintings were donated to the creation evidence museum located in Glenrose, Texas.

In the year 2008 starting with the month of January I started painting the WWII mural titled, "WWII Memorial." The mural was 6'x9' on canvas and framed with oakwood. It was donated along with a $500 gift for the charity to the Utica center for Development in December 2008. The charitable orginaztion was founded by executive director Vincent Scalise, who founded the center whose humanitarian objective was to provide a facility for the homeless and veterans with food and shelter for the needy. He organized a team of workers and set about rehab of the old YMCA building that had been vacant for over ten years and was in almost complete ruin. It took him and his men working without time out to renovate the building. I contacted director Scalise and he was pleased for some decaration with honoring the veterans that fought in the defence of America. I delivered the mural and it was installed in the hallway of the center in early 2009, and dedicated there at Utica, NY.

WWII was the worst war in history. America entered as a result of the attack on Pearl Harbor. Over 475,000 military personnel from America; lost their lives. I chose to alter the perspective to reveal more of the landscape and labeled the pillars that represented the states of the union and provinces. The mural was 9 feet high by 6 ½ feet wide. It took me three months to complete in the year 2008. He used two picture frames to show the WWII battles and famous quotations.

In the year 2009 I painted the Korean War Memorial, the raising the flag on Iwo Jima, the battle of Midway, and the sea to shining sea painting these paintings were all mounted in the Utica Development center.

In April 2007 I sent a portrait to the curator of the Marilyn Monroe Museum in Archangel, Russia. The curator prized it and it became a major feature of the museum's collection.

My latest painting project is painting the portraits of eleven famous musicians. These are similar to the ones I sent to the Philadelphia academy of music in April 2008.

Todays mathematicians, astronomers and scientists are working on theories of evolution, our schools, colleges and universities all seem to be stuck on the evolution theory and shy away from creation.

The big bang theory has been questioned, where did all the elements come from? All the bang made was mostly hydrogen and helium. I think God spoke them to be made from his own creation.

A creator should be able to tell us how life appeared and wheather life has a purpose. Questions that science is incapable of answering. These questions are addressed by the writings called the bible or the Holy scriptures, whose writers claimed to be inspired by the Creator, consider what the bible says.

I prefer a Veterains Administration (VA) burial with headstone and a 21 gun salute that the VA has provided us servicemen who put their lives on the line during modern conflicts.

WESTWARD-HO MURAL
SIZE: 5' X 8' OIL
ARTIST: JOHN R. HUCKABY
LOCATED: CENTRAL WYOMING COLLEGE, RIVERTON WY.

CREATION STORY
SIZE 6' X 8' OIL
ARTIST: JOHN R. HUCKABY
LOCATED: CREATION EVIDENCE MUSEUM, GLEN ROSE, TX.

ThE CRUCIFIXION OF JESUS
SIZE: 5' X 6' OIL
ARTIST: JOhN R. hUCKABY
LOCATED: ST. VOLODYMR THE GREAT UKRANIAN CATHOLIC ChURCh, UTICA, NY.

ABRAHAM LEAVES UR OF CHALDEANS MURAL
SIZE: 5' X 6' OIL
ARTIST: JOHN R. HUCKABY
LOCATED: ST. VOLODYMR THE GREAT UKRANIAN CATHOLIC CHURCH, UTICA, NY.

PAINTING, A WONDERFUL THERAPY

Afraid to start? Do you know everyone is, even professionals are from time to time, but have a job that must be out, next Wednesday and get at it because they may have a family that has gotten into the habit of eating three times a day or the payment on the house or car may be coming up? So it is a must for the professional but you may be painting for fun so this fear of making a mistake has a greater influence over you and you may say to yourself "I'm not inspired today" or I don't think I have a talent for painting, or a dozen other excuses one can make to get out of starting. Another great mis-Today's mathematicians, astronomers and scientist are working on theories of evolution, our schools, colleges and universities all seem to be stuck on the evolution theory and shy away from creation.

The big bang theory has been questioned, where did all the elements come from? All the bang made was mostly hydrogen and helium. I think God spoke them to be made from his own creation.

A creator should be able to tell us how life appeared and whether life has a purpose. Questions that science is incapable of answering these questions are addressed by the writings called the bible or the Holy Scriptures, whose writers claimed to be inspired by the creator, consider what the bible says.

I prefer a veterans administration (VA) burial with headstone and a 21 gun salute that the VA has provided for us servicemen who put their lives on the line during modern conflicts. John's remarkable progress as an artist has been noted by both the official art world and the general public. For many years now at the age of 90, he has explored the teachings of the masters and in his own work he has successfully brought together the best elements of both the traditional and modern schools of painting. The principles of portraiture that he understands, discuses and demonstrates are those he teaches and practices in his own paintings.

APPENDIX #1

JOHN HUCKABY: COMPLETED ULTRA MARATHONS, MARATHONS

DATE	ULTRA-MARATHON, MARATHON	LOCATION	DISTANCE
3/20/77	Boston Qualifier Marathon	Rome, NY/Oneida, NY	26.2 M
10/22/77	Skylon Marathon	Buffalo, Niagara Falls	26.2 M
12/8/77	Jersey Shore Marathon	Asbury Park, NJ	26.2 M
3/5/78	Heart Marathon	Rome/Oneida, NY	26.2 M
3/18/78	Schenetedy Marathon	Schenetedy, NY	26.2 M
4/17/78	Boston Marathon	Boston, Mass.	26.2 M
5/20/78	Platsburg Marathon	Platsburg, NY	26.2 M
9/17/78	Adam Helmer Marathon	Skyler Lake, NY	26.2 M
9/30/78	Old Forge Marathon	Old Forge, NY	26.2 M
10/8/78	Finger Lake Marathon	Canandaugwa, NY	26.2 M
10/21/78	Skylon Marathon	Buffalo, Niagara Falls	26.2 M
10/22/78	NY City Marathon (back to back)	New York City, NY	26.2 M
11/18/78	JFK Memorial Ultra-marathon	Boonsborough, MD	50.2 M
12/2/78	Jersey Shore Marathon	Asbury Park, NJ	26.2 M
12/10/78	Cape Cod Marathon	Otis AFB, Mass.	26.2 M
4/16/79	Boston Marathon	Boston, Mass	26.2 M
1/27/79	Mayor Juiler Ultra-Marathon	Miami, Fl	62.2 M
3/4/79	Heart Marathon	Rome, NY/Oneida, NY	26.2 M
5/6/79	Lake Waramaug Ultra Marathon	Lake Waramaug, Conn	50.0 M
5/22/79	Athens International Marathon (3 times nonstop)	Athens, Greece	78.6 M
7/8/79	Western States Ultra-Marathon	Squaw Vatiey to Auburn Ca.	100.0M
9/3/79	Rochester Marathon	Rochester, NY	26.2 M
9/8/79	Presque Isle, Marathon	Presque Is., Penn	26.2 M
9/15/79	Lake Placid Marathon	Lake Placid, NY	26.2 M
9/17/79	Adam Helmer Marathon	Schuler Lake, NY	26.2 M
10/6/79	Frankfort to Louisville Ultra	Louisville, KY	50 M
10/13/79	Sklon Marathon	Buffalo/Niagara Falls	26.2 M
10/28/79	Allentown Ultra	Allentown, Pa.	50 M
11/3/79	Harrisburg Marathon	Harrisburg, Pa	26.2 M
11/17/79	John F. Kennedy Ultra-Marathon	Boonsborough, Pa	50.2M
12/2/79	Jersey Shore Marathon	Asbury Park, NJ	26.2 M
1/12/80	Hawaiian Triathlon	Honolulu, Hi	140.6M
2/10/80	New Orleans Marathon	Ponchertrain Bridge	26.2 M

4/6/80	Ardmore, Okla Ultra-Marathon	Ardmore, OK	42 M
4/20/80	Boston Protest Ultra-Marathon	Boston, Mas	104.8M
5/4/80	Lake Waramaug Ultra-Marathon	New Preston, Conn	50 M
5/11/80	Ottawa Marathon	Ottawa, Canada	26.2 M
5/25/80	Philadelphia to Atlantic city Ultra-Marathon	Phil., Pa; Atlantic City, NJ	62.2M
7/20/80	Volksmarchen Ultra-Marathon	Ramstein, Germany (TDY)	80 KM
7/22/80	Adana Turkey trot Ultra-Marathon	Adana-Kozan, Turkey (TDY)	80 KM
10/31/80	Goblin Gallup 12hr/24hr, 2,5m, 10km	Memphis, Tenn	109 M
8/2/80	Adirondack Marathon	Star Lake, NY	26.2 M
8/17/80	Empire State Marathon	Syracuse, NY	26.2 M
9/1/80	Rochester Marathon	Rochester, NY	26.2 M
9/14/80	Schuler Marathon (Adam Helmer)	Shuler Lake, NY	26.2 M
9/20/80	Biathlon Ultra-Marathon	Rome, NY-Johnstown, NY	78 M
9/28/80	Autumn Leaves Marathon	Old Forge, NY	26.2 M
10/26/80	New York City Marathon	New York City, NY	26.2 M
11/23/80	Providence Rhode Island Marathon	Providence, RI	26.2 M
11/30/80	Philadelphia Marathon	Philadelphia, PA	26.2 M
12/6/80	Penn state Marathon	Penn State	26.2 M
12/7/80	Asbury Park Marathon (back to back)	Asbury Park, NJ	26.2 M
4/17-20/81	Albany - Boston Odyssey Ultra-Marathon	Albany, NY-Boston, Ma	205 M
5/3/81	Lake Waramaug Ultra-Marathon	New Preston, Conn	50 M
6/13/81	Laurat Highlands Ultra-Marathon	Johnstown, PA	56 M
7/5/81	Midnight sun Ultra-Marathon	Nanisivik Arctic Bay, NWT	52.4 M
	(Double Marathon 400 miles above Arctic Circle)		
10/4/81	AMJA Ultra-Marathon	Chicago, Il	100K
	John Huckaby RRCA national champ age 60 plus		
11/4/81	Nickel City Fifty Miler Ultra-Marathon	Buffalo, NY	50 M
11/21/81	Marrion Corrigan 24 Hour run	Auburn, NY	101 M + 753 yds.
	(John Huckaby national Champ 24 hours & 100 miles)		
	(ran 1,088 laps plus 43 on 150M certified trac)		
11/28/81	Philadelphia Marathon	Philadelphia, PA	26.2 M
4/19/82	Boston Marathon	Boston, Mass	26.2 M
5/16/82	Liverpool Marathon	Liverpool, NY	26.2 M
5/29/82	Waterloo Marathon	Waterloo, NY	26.2 M
6/27-7/1/82	Pennsauken 6 day Ultra-marathon	Pennsauken, NJ	203.8 M
7/4/82	Star Lake Marathon	StarLake, NY	26.2 M
7/9/82	Rochester Marathon	Rochester, NY	26.2 M
9/9/82	Adam Helmer Marathon	Schyler Lake, NY	26.2 M
10/25/82	Old Forge Marathon	Old Forge, NY	26.2 M
10/3/82	Canandaigua Lake Ultra Marathon	Canandaigua, NY	60KM
10/21-24/82	Montauk to Manhattan Ultra Marathon	Montauk, LI-Manhattan, NY	159.2M
11/7/82	Erie Canal Ultra-Marathon	Syracuse NY-Rome, NY	41 M
11/28/82	Philadelphia Marathon	Philadelphia, PA	26.2 M
11/21/82	J.F.K. Ultra Marathon	Boonsbrough, MD	50.2 M
3/16-17/83	Boston marathon Qualifier marathon	Rome, NY	26.2 M
4/17/83	Boston Marathon	Boston, Mass	26.2 M
5/15/83	Ottawa International Marathon	Ottawa, Canada	26.0 M (DNF)
5/15/83	Heart Attack; Huck's Racing Career Finished (.2M short of finish)		

APPENDIX #2

John R. Huckaby's wartime and cold war experiences

Age 90

USS WM P. BIDDEL
Prior Pearl Harbor
Iceland
1 landing 6th marines May 1941
1 landing army August 1941
USS Harris APA 2
After Pearl Harbor (In route Pearl Harbor; arrived Dec 25, what a mess)

Honolulu
2 trips evacuating dependents 1 Jan 1942
1 trip transporting nurses Feb 1942
Amphibious landings Atlantic
1 landing Casablanca with Pattom RM3c and Safi, Morocco 8 Nov 1942
Amphibious Landings Pacific
1 landing Wallis Island July 1942-June 4, 1942 Battle of midway
1 landing Entiwetok
1 landing Kwjalein Dec 4, 1943
1 landing Attu May 13, 1943
1 landing Kiska (Japanese abandoned one day prior invasion)
1 landing Saipan 1944
1 landing Tinian 1944
1 landing Pelilu 1944
1 landing Tarawa (one of the bloodiest battles I was ever in)
1 landing Magmag
1 landing Anguar Ulithi 1944
1 landing Leyte with MacArthur Oct 12, 1944
1 landing Zamboles, Philippine Islands 1945
1 landing Okinawa (chief petty officer) radio hit beach okinawa 4/1/45
1 landing Lynguyen Gulf 1 Nov 1944 Attacked by kamakaza suiside bombers april fools day
1 landing reinforcement Iwo Jima summer 1945. Atomic bomb dropped on Nagasaki and Hiroshima 6th and 19th August 1945. Japan surrendered August 20th 1945 and WWII ended

KOREAN WAR
USS LSMR 403 ROCKET LAUNCHING SHIP 2 ½ Yrs. Chief Radioman.
Inchon Bombarding East Coast Korea and West at Sonjin.

Sonjin Bombarding West Coast Korea above 38th Paralell.
Holding Wonampondo Island from occupation

VIETNAM (FRENCH) 1954
Soul Radio Officer on merchant ship US ANTHONY ran war cargo from Marseilles, France to Saigon, Indo China. Manned 50 Cal. Machine Gun 50 miles to Saigon under sniper fire.

US AIR BASES IN FRANCE 1955-57
Installed/operated/maintained 24 Chan. Microwave System from Fountainbleau center France to England with tiein Germany and Bordeau. (The cold war was warming up)

SAUDIARABIA 1958
Leaving Beruth airport the airplane (ARAMCO) was attacked on runway as plane was leaving with me and other engineers aboard morter shells were landing on runway just behind takeoff.

NATIONAL AND INTERNATIONAL SECURITY 1970-85

Fifteen years protecting America and our Alies during the cold war era.

****

APENDIX #3

John R. Huckaby and Family Photographs/ages

John R. Huckaby Sr. 91
Betty M. Huckaby 88
John R. Huckaby Jr. 69
Nanci HuckabyPeroni 55

John's wife Betty, son Jr. and John Sr.

John Sr. Son John Jr., daughter Nanci Peroni

Brother and Sister, John R. Huckaby Jr. and Nanci Huckaby Peroni

Poopoo, John and Betty

John's Painting of Jesus, Betty and her Cat Patches.

Printed by Publishers' Graphics LLC
PGD-07598